DEC -- 2020

W9-BEL-147

WITHDRAWN
Woodridge Public Library

CULTURES OF THE WORLD

North Macedonia

Cavendish
Square
New York

WOODRIDGE PUBLIC LIBRARY
Three Plaza Drive
Woodridge, IL 60517-5014

Published in 2021 by Cavendish Square Publishing, LLC
243 5th Avenue, Suite 136, New York, NY 10016

Copyright © 2021 by Cavendish Square Publishing, LLC

Third Edition

No part of this publication may be reproduced, stored in a retrieval system, or transmitted in any form or by any means—electronic, mechanical, photocopying, recording, or otherwise—without the prior permission of the copyright owner. Request for permission should be addressed to Permissions, Cavendish Square Publishing, 243 5th Avenue, Suite 136, New York, NY 10016. Tel (877) 980-4450; fax (877) 980-4454.

Website: cavendishsq.com

This publication represents the opinions and views of the author based on his or her personal experience, knowledge, and research. The information in this book serves as a general guide only. The author and publisher have used their best efforts in preparing this book and disclaim liability rising directly or indirectly from the use and application of this book.

All websites were available and accurate when this book was sent to press.

Library of Congress Cataloging-in-Publication Data

Names: Knowlton, Mary Lee, 1946- author. | Nevins, Debbie, author.
Title: North Macedonia / Mary L. Knowlton, Debbie Nevins.
Description: Third edition. | New York : Cavendish Square Publishing, 2021.
 | Series: Cultures of the world | Includes bibliographical references
 and index.
Identifiers: LCCN 2019049690 (print) | LCCN 2019049691 (ebook) | ISBN
 9781502655899 (library binding) | ISBN 9781502655905 (ebook)
Subjects: LCSH: North Macedonia--Juvenile literature.
Classification: LCC DR2160 .K6 2021 (print) | LCC DR2160 (ebook) | DDC
 949.76--dc23
LC record available at https://lccn.loc.gov/2019049690
LC ebook record available at https://lccn.loc.gov/2019049691

Editor, third edition: Debbie Nevins
Designer, third edition: Jessica Nevins

The photographs in this book are used with the permission of: Cover Hriana/Shutterstock.com; p. 1 RossHelen/Shutterstock.com; p. 3 Robert Zahariev/Shutterstock.com; p. 5 Thomas Dekiere/Shutterstock.com; pp. 6, 7, 24 Peter Hermes Furian/Shutterstock.com; p. 8 Zvonimir Atletic/Shutterstock.com; pp. 10, 94 Aybige Mert/Shutterstock.com; p. 12 corgarashu/Shutterstock.com; p. 13 Milos Djokic/Shutterstock.com; p. 14 trabantos/Shutterstock.com; p. 16 TPGryf/Shutterstock.com; p. 18 Kanuman/Shutterstock.com; pp. 19, 128 Eric Valenne geostory/Shutterstock.com; pp. 20, 48, 74 Sarnia/Shutterstock.com; p. 21 Jetmir Sejdija/Shutterstock.com; p. 22 boris zhrchvich/Shutterstock.com; pp. 25, 107 bumihills/Shutterstock.com; pp. 26, 101 ColorMaker/Shutterstock.com; p. 30 Ulrich Baumgarten via Getty Images; p. 31 pablofdezr/Shutterstock.com; p. 32 Future Perfect at Sunrise/File:Macedonia overview.svg/Wikimedia Commons/CC_PD-self; p. 34 stoyanh/Shutterstock.com; pp. 36, 38, 61, 64, 71, 100, 118 ROBERT ATANASOVSKI/AFP/Getty Images; p. 39 Alexandros Michailidis/Shutterstock.com; p. 40 photosmatic/Shutterstock.com; p. 42 Giovanni Vale/Shutterstock.com; p. 44 Adriana Iacob/Shutterstock.com; p. 50 cuckove/Shutterstock.com; p. 52 MAVRITSINA IRINA/Shutterstock.com; pp. 56, 58, 70, 72 Neil Bussey/Shutterstock.com; p. 59 Filip Viranovski/Shutterstock.com; pp. 60, 65 Roula St Kaba/Shutterstock.com; p. 62 mark reinstein/Shutterstock.com; p. 66 V.Lawrence/Shutterstock.com; p. 68 Dimitar Popov/Shutterstock.com; p. 73 Daniela Jovanovska-Hristovska/E+/Getty Images; p. 75 Djordje Novakov/Shutterstock.com; p. 76 stefan dzalev/Shutterstock.com; p. 78 risteski goce/Shutterstock.com; p. 80 S-F/Shutterstock.com; p. 81 Drop of Light/Shutterstock.com; pp. 82, 103, 114, 117, 127 agrofruti/Shutterstock.com; p. 83 marcovarro/Shutterstock.com; p. 84 bumihills/Shutterstock.com; p. 85 Zoran Karapancev/Shutterstock.com; p. 86 leszczem/Shutterstock.com; p. 88 YKD/Shutterstock.com; p. 90 fritz16/Shutterstock.com; p. 92 ArnoldPlaton/Wikimedia Commons/File:Albanian dialects.svg/ CC BY-SA 3.0; p. 96 Fco. Lozano Alcobendas/Shutterstock.com; p. 97 saiko3p/Shutterstock.com; p. 98 Делфина/Wikimedia Commons/File:Christian religious buildings 169.JPG/CC BY-SA 3.0; p. 102 capa55/Shutterstock.com; p. 104 (top) R R/Shutterstock.com; p. 104 (bottom) Bobica10/Shutterstock.com; p. 105 Ilya S. Savenok/Getty Images; pp. 106, 112 zefart/Shutterstock.com; p. 108 Atosan/Shutterstock.com; p. 110 Igor Panevski/Shutterstock.com; p. 111 Ljupco Smokovski/Shutterstock.com; p. 116 Munzir Rosdi/Shutterstock.com; p. 119 roibu/Shutterstock.com; p. 121 NurPhoto/Corbis via Getty Images; p. 124 nada54/Shutterstock.com; p. 126 Pe3k/Shutterstock.com; p. 129 Dreamsquare/Shutterstock.com; p. 130 AS Food studio/Shutterstock.com; p. 131 NoirChocolate/Shutterstock.com

Some of the images in this book illustrate individuals who are models. The depictions do not imply actual situations or events.

CPSIA compliance information: Batch #CS20CSQ: For further information contact Cavendish Square Publishing LLC, New York, New York, at 1-877-980-4450.

Printed in the United States of America

CONTENTS

NORTH MACEDONIA TODAY

NORTH MACEDONIA IS A NEW NAME FOR AN OLD PLACE. IT HAS had a number of different names over the centuries. How does a country change its name? In this most recent case, after years of discussion—some would say bickering—what was once the Republic of Macedonia passed a constitutional amendment and, beginning in 2019, became the Republic of North Macedonia.

Why does a country change its name? That's a longer story, and it's told in the History and Government chapters of this book. Spoiler alert: It has much to do with ancient history, national identity, an unhappy neighbor, and a dream for the future.

North Macedonia is not one of those countries that gets much coverage in the American press. In fact, many Americans would probably have trouble finding it on a map, if they've heard of it at all. North Macedonia may be relatively small, but as a civilization it has been around, in one form or another, almost forever. Skopje (SKOH-pee-ah), its capital, is at least 6,000 years old.

The country is located in southeastern Europe, in a region called the Balkans. The Balkan Peninsula extends to the south of continental Europe, bounded to the west by the Adriatic Sea, to the south by the Ionian and Aegean Seas, and to the east

This map of North Macedonia shows its important cities, rivers, lakes, and borders with surrounding countries.

by the Black Sea. The region itself is surrounded by water on three sides, as peninsulas are, but for all those seas, North Macedonia has no coast at all. It's a landlocked country located more or less in the center of the great peninsular landmass, where it's surrounded by less-than-friendly neighbors. It is relatively small, though not tiny—about the size of Vermont or New Hampshire—and is a sort of rounded nugget shape. A map of North Macedonia would be much easier to draw than, say, a map of its neighbor to the south, Greece, with its highly irregular coastline and its thousands of islands.

Greece, for its part, has been a thorn in the side of its northern neighbor ever since what was then called simply Macedonia first proclaimed independence in 1991. That story is told later in these pages as well. Essentially, the problem between them all comes down to the question, "Will the real Macedonia please stand up?" It's a question that found both Greece and Macedonia standing up, nose to nose, fists up, and ready to battle it out.

North Macedonia, therefore, might be said to have an identity problem. This is hinted at in the great name change of 2019, but it involves more than just a label. History has defined the place and its people in many ways, but today, North Macedonia struggles to figure out just what kind of country it is and what it wants to be.

Is it the great homeland of the ethnic Macedonian people, with legendary, even mythological, ties to the ancient Kingdom of Macedon and its exalted hero, Alexander the Great? Is it a modern, multiethnic, multilingual nation of Christians and Muslims who somehow find unity under the North Macedonian flag? Is it a former communist country that should now look to Russia and the East for its political, economic, and cultural guidance, or is it a European country that awaits the embrace of the Western European community at large?

The yellow area roughly describes the geographical region called Macedonia.

Pope Francis celebrates a Roman Catholic mass outdoors in Skopje's Macedonia Square during his May 2019 visit to North Macedonia.

When Pope Francis, head of the Roman Catholic Church, visited North Macedonia in May 2019, he called attention to the question of identity. He praised North Macedonia as "a bridge between the East and West." That is very much the case, but a bridge is a tough thing to be. It is neither here nor there, and with too heavy a burden, a bridge can collapse.

Pope Francis's visit—the first ever by a pope—epitomized the same idea. The Catholic Church itself is divided into East and West, a schism that has lasted a thousand years. North Macedonia is an Eastern Orthodox Catholic country; there are very few Roman Catholics (the Western branch of the Church). However, the country is nonetheless the homeland of one of the world's most beloved contemporary Roman Catholics—the woman known as Mother Teresa, who was born in Skopje in 1910. She died in 1997, and Pope

Francis himself canonized her (designated her a saint) in 2016. In a further expression of the country's ethnic complexity, she was also Albanian. Ethnic Albanians are the largest ethnic minority in North Macedonia—an aggrieved minority at that—and most of them, unlike Teresa, are Muslim.

During his quick visit, the pope urged the people of North Macedonia to come together in unity. He called the country "a mosaic in which every piece is essential for the uniqueness and beauty of the whole." That is ideally the country's goal.

Another is to be brought into the European family, by way of acceptance into the European Union (EU). That has been the dream, with economic benefits, political stability, and a secure national identity as the expected reward. So it was a shock when, on October 17, 2019, the EU's European Council voted not to grant North Macedonia a date to start what are called accession talks. Essentially, the EU shut its door in the face of the hopeful country, leading to outrage and disappointment. North Macedonia's angriest citizen may have been its prime minister, Zoran Zaev, who had staked his political career on EU acceptance. After all, a large part of the nation's name change had been undertaken so that it could apply for EU membership. With the sound of the slamming door still ringing metaphorically in the air, Zaev called for early elections and stepped down as prime minister.

North Macedonia's future, therefore, is up in the air, but there seems to be reason to be hopeful. One of the nation's official symbols is a bright yellow sun—it is emblazoned on the national flag. Another is a lion—the Macedonian lion. Together, they stand for optimism and strength, a good omen for an ancient place yearning for a bright future.

GEOGRAPHY

The beautiful Matka Canyon is a popular outdoor destination in North Macedonia.

1

OVER THE COURSE OF HISTORY, THE name Macedonia has described a variety of places. From the ancient Kingdom of Macedon to the Greek province, the Roman province, and the geographical region, and on from there to the modern nation, Macedonia's boundaries have shifted. All have spanned more or less of the south-central Balkan Peninsula. Today, the Republic of North Macedonia, which until 2019 was the Republic of Macedonia, comprises a part of historic and geographic Macedonia.

It is a small, landlocked country on the Balkan Peninsula in southeastern Europe, which it shares with Albania, Greece, and the nations that once made up the former Yugoslavia, which broke apart in 1991. Just slightly larger than the state of Vermont, it has an area of 9,928 square miles (25,713 square kilometers). It is bordered by Albania to the west and Greece to the south. In the north, it borders Kosovo and Serbia, and in the east, Bulgaria.

The Matka Canyon on the Treska River is a scenic tourist and recreation destination in North Macedonia. It is home to several medieval monasteries built into the rock and 10 underwater caves. The deepest, Cave Vrelo, with an estimated depth of 755 feet (230 meters), is filled with stalactites and is only accessible by boat.

The rocky peak of Mount Korab towers above the mountain range of the same name. Mount Korab itself spans the border of Albania and North Macedonia.

MOUNTAINS

North Macedonia is a mountainous country, with 34 peaks that are higher than 6,562 feet (2,000 m). The tallest is Mount Korab at 9,069 feet (2,764 m) above sea level. In the Sar Planina mountain range, Titov Vrv is 9,016 feet (2,748 m) high, and Turchin reaches 8,865 feet (2,702 m).

Titov Vrv means "Tito's Mountain," and was named after (and by) the former leader of Yugoslavia. Though it is the second-highest mountain in North Macedonia, it is the highest mountain lying completely within the country, which is why it was picked to honor Tito.

WATERWAYS

The Vardar is North Macedonia's most significant river in both size and history, cutting across the middle of the country for 187 miles (301 km) from the

northwest to the southeast before flowing into Greece and emptying into the Aegean Sea. The Treska and Crna Rivers join the Vardar on its way south through the country—the Treska at Skopje and the Crna farther south.

North Macedonia has 53 natural or artificial lakes. Lake Ohrid (AW-rid or AWK-rid) in the southwest, with a depth of 938 feet (286 m), is the deepest lake on the Balkan Peninsula and straddles the border of North Macedonia and Albania. Of its area of 130 square miles (340 sq km), about one-third belongs to Albania. Over 3 million years old, Lake Ohrid is often called a museum of living fossils. Lake Ohrid is largely a spring-fed lake, drawing its waters from deep underground rather than from contributory rivers. Its waters are fully replaced only every 60 or 70 years, which makes it particularly vulnerable to damage by pollution.

The lake is home to numerous endemic species (those found nowhere else on Earth), including the endangered Ohrid trout, a fish from the Tertiary period of geological history. The lake is also the only sanctuary for other endangered

City lights twinkle in the early evening, reflecting in the Vardar River as it flows through Skopje. The permanently moored clipper ship is a casino. In the background, the lights of the new Art Bridge span the river, and the white structures to the left are new government office buildings.

The red roofs of Ohrid contrast with the blue waters of the famous lake of the same name.

fish that exist only in fossil form in other parts of the world where they became extinct during the last Ice Age. Overfishing and pollution have increased the peril for these rare creatures.

Lake Prespa, a little farther south, spans parts of North Macedonia, Albania, and Greece. Lake Dojran, also known as Doiran Lake, in the southeast, is on the Greek border.

CLIMATE

North Macedonia is a country of hot, dry summers and falls. Its winters, though snowy between November and February, are warmer than those of its northern neighbors, thanks to the moderating Aegean winds that blow from the south through the Vardar River valley. Still, in the mountainous areas, farmers can see snow on the mountain peaks when they plant their seeds in the warmer valleys in the spring.

WORLD HERITAGE SITES

Since 1975, the United Nations Educational, Scientific and Cultural Organization (UNESCO) has maintained a list of international landmarks or regions considered to be of "outstanding value" to the people of the world. Such sites embody the common natural and cultural heritage of humanity and therefore deserve particular protection. The organization works with the host country to establish plans for managing and conserving their sites. UNESCO also reports on sites which are in imminent or potential danger of destruction and can offer emergency funds to try to save the property.

The organization is continually assessing new sites for inclusion on the World Heritage list. In order to be selected, a site must be of "outstanding universal value" and meet at least one of ten criteria. These required elements include cultural value—that is, artistic, religious, or historical significance—and natural value, including exceptional beauty, unusual natural phenomenon, or scientific importance.

As of January 2020, there were 1,121 sites listed, including 869 cultural, 213 natural, and 39 mixed (cultural and natural) properties in 167 nations. Of those, 53 were listed as "in danger."

North Macedonia's only UNESCO World Heritage site is the Lake Ohrid region, which is noted for both its natural and cultural features. In 2019, the site was extended to include the Albanian part of the lake.

In 2019, concerns over the environmental deterioration of the lakeside town of Ohrid prompted UNESCO to recommend reclassifying the site as "endangered," a mark that many countries would like to avoid. With its ancient and beautiful churches, houses, and monuments, Ohrid contributes much of what constitutes the site's cultural heritage.

This wasn't the first time the World Heritage body identified concerns about the region. In April 2017, it listed a wide range of pressures, including road construction, traffic, tourism development, overfishing, sewage, solid waste disposal, invasive species, legal and illegal construction, and management of water levels. The governing body issued a report listing 19 recommendations for preserving the site's natural and cultural integrity.

NATIONAL PARKS

North Macedonia has three national parks, all in the western part of the country. Galicica National Park comprises about 88 square miles (227 sq km) of land between Lake Ohrid and Lake Prespa, and is dominated by Mount Galicica. To the east of Lake Prespa is Pelister National Park, the country's oldest park, which takes up about 66 square miles (171.5 sq km). North of the city of Debar, on the Albanian border, is Mavrovo National Park, by far the country's largest park, spanning 301 square miles (780 sq km).

The best-known summer resorts are in Ohrid, Prespa, and Dojran. In winter, the mountain resorts of Popova Shapka, Mavrovo, Pelister, Krushevo, and Ponikva draw skiers from all over Europe. Among the better known spas are those of Bansko (Strumica), Debar, Negorci (Gevgelija), and Kechovica (Shtip).

Lake Prespa can be seen in the distance from Pelister National Park.

LAND USE

Nearly 40 percent of the land of North Macedonia is forested, and 44.3 percent is agricultural land, more than half of which is pastureland. Over 70 percent of the arable land is privately owned, mostly in small parcels.

North Macedonia is a country of avid hunters, who hunt deer, bears, hares, boars, partridges, and pheasants. Hunting grounds and reserves are set aside for hunters.

FLORA AND FAUNA

North Macedonia is a land of forests. In the mountain regions, beech and chestnut trees grow in the lower elevations. Above 3,940 feet (1,200 m), conifers prevail, mostly fir and pine. Around Lakes Ohrid and Prespa, cypress, walnut, and fig trees grow.

The forests are home to deer, martens, and wild boars. In the mountains, there are bears, ibexes, lynx, and chamois. The western lake district has a wide variety of fish and waterfowl, including cormorants, the Ohrid trout, and pelicans.

CITIES

SKOPJE   North Macedonia's capital and largest city, with a population of about 590,000, is located in the north of the country in a valley on the Vardar River. Skopje has been an urban settlement since around 500 BCE and long ago served several civilizations as the intersection of two major trading routes.

The Vardar divides the city into ethnic communities, the Muslim section on the north bank and the Orthodox Christian section on the south. The Muslim section of town, the old city, has a traditional Turkish bazaar every day, where people can buy fresh foods in season and Macedonian crafts. The southern part of the city contains the buildings of the government as well as shopping malls and modern hotels.

The architecture of Skopje reflects its numerous rulers, who embarked on building projects each time the city changed hands. Beautiful old mosques,

An aerial view reveals the beauty of Macedonia Square in central Skopje.

a stone bridge known as Kameni Most, and medieval Turkish baths have survived floods and earthquakes. An earthquake in 1963, which left more than 1,000 people dead and 100,000 homeless, destroyed most of the city's 18th- and 19th-century buildings in the southern part of the city, while sparing the Turkish buildings in the north.

The church and monastery of Sveti Spas, which means "holy salvation," has survived both earthquakes and communism as the only remaining monastery in Skopje. Parts of the church date to the 14th century, and additions and repairs extended into the 19th. During the 400 years of Ottoman rule, a church could not be built taller than a mosque, so the additions to Sveti Spas were built underground.

OHRID   The city of Ohrid is a treasure not only to North Macedonia but to the rest of the world as well. Cultural and environmental importance has earned both the city and the lake on which it is located UNESCO protection. As one of the world's oldest lakes, Lake Ohrid needs protection because of its supply of ancient and rare animal life. The city itself has an ancient history as well, stretching back to prehistoric times, around 6000 BCE. Once known as Lihnidos, meaning "City of Light," Ohrid has been home to most of the important peoples of the area, including Illyrians, Greeks, and Romans, as well as Macedonians.

At the end of the ninth century, it was renamed Ohrid, meaning "City of a Hill," by the Slavs, who had taken control. Since then, Ohrid has been the heart of Macedonia, originating its written language, its first university, its church, and many of its rebellions against invaders and occupiers. In 1466, the citizens

Browsers walk the charming streets of Ohrid in the summertime.

A gentle river runs beside a street on the outskirts of Bitola.

of Ohrid sided with the Albanians and their leader, George Skanderbeg, in their revolt against the Ottoman Empire. Though the revolt was ultimately put down, the effort was a noble one, and Macedonians of Albanian descent in Ohrid still cherish Skanderbeg's memory.

Throughout the city of Ohrid, its history as a trading hub and a center of many civilizations is evident in the architecture that remains, sometimes in ruin, but treasured nevertheless. The Church of Saint Sophia illustrates a history typical of Macedonia. In the early 11th century, it was built as a cathedral for the archbishop on the remains of a former basilica. Under the Ottomans, it was transformed into a mosque, and later, though still during the Ottoman Empire, it became a warehouse. In 1912, it became, once again, a church. In its incarnation as a cathedral, the church was lavishly decorated with frescoes on its walls and ceiling. As Islam forbids human representation, the frescoes were painted over during the building's mosque incarnation, and so they remained until the 20th century, when they were restored to their original beauty.

Ohrid is very much a lake community, and people get around by boat taxi as well as car and bus. In summer, it is host to the Ohrid International Swimming Marathon, a 19-mile (30 km) race from Saint Naum on the Albanian border to this city.

BITOLA   Bitola is Macedonia's second-largest city, with a population of 74,500 people. It is in the south of the country and was a stop on the Via Egnatia, the Roman road that connected Constantinople (now Istanbul) with Rome. It was founded by the father of Alexander the Great, and at one time, every European country of importance had a consulate there. It has since lost much of its international glory, but it retains its cultural significance, which is evident in the buildings that are well preserved throughout the city. Bitola was central to the Ilinden Uprising in 1903 as the training center for guerrillas. During the brutal reprisals that the Turks visited upon the Macedonians after

The city of Tetovo glows at night, surrounded by dark mountains.

the uprising was subdued, the Manaki brothers, Janaki and Milton, established a photography studio in Bitola and recorded for all the world to see the violence of those years and of the Balkan Wars that followed in 1912 and 1913.

TETOVO Tetovo is in the northwestern part of Macedonia, not far from Kosovo and Albania at the foot of the towering Mount Titov Vrv. With a majority Albanian population, it's the most important Albanian city in North Macedonia and is the headquarters for the Albanian political parties. The language of the streets and shops is Albanian, and though Macedonian is spoken, it is not favored.

INTERNET LINKS

https://www.nytimes.com/2019/05/17/travel/republic-of-north -macedonia-balkans.html
This travel article is a quick overview of the country, with an explanation of its name change.

https://whc.unesco.org/en/list/99
The UNESCO World Heritage Centre website describes the "Natural and Cultural Heritage of the Ohrid Region."

HISTORY

This tall statue of Alexander the Great was erected in 2011 in Skopje to both cheers and jeers. Critics say it's too large for its surroundings and is a provocation to Greece.

2

NORTH MACEDONIA IS A NEW NAME for an ancient place. The small country takes its name from what was once a vast empire, and over the centuries it has been home to peoples of varying ethnicities, creeds, and traditions. All of that long and complicated history still courses through the country today. It can be seen in the lay of the land and in the culture, languages, and identities of the North Macedonian people.

Historically, Macedonia is closely identified with the kingdom of Philip II of Macedon, who ruled during the fourth century BCE. His son Alexander III, otherwise known to the world as Alexander the Great, expanded the empire to its greatest extent, far beyond the borders of today's small Republic of North Macedonia.

ANCIENT ORIGINS

Early Greek writers describe a legendary country called Paeonia that stretched the length of the Vardar River, from its origins in the mountains of the north through today's Greece to the Aegean Sea.

According to the ancient writer Homer, the Paeons were descended from Axios, the Greek river god, and were participants in the Trojan War. The Paeons and neighboring tribes, who were the ancestors of Greeks, Albanians, Bulgarians, and Serbs, fought alongside and against each other in the Balkans for centuries. The remains of their walled cities can be found throughout North Macedonia. Their civilization, the first in the area, flourished between 7000 and 3500 BCE.

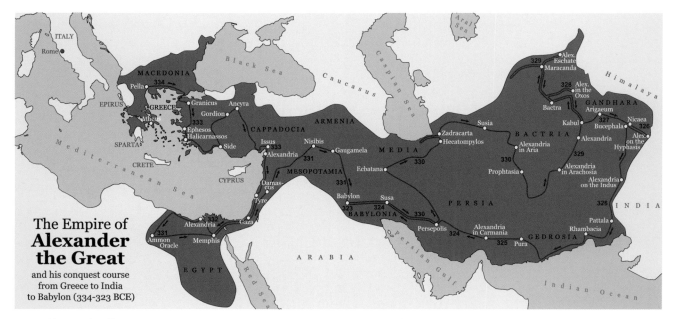

The Empire of
**Alexander
the Great**
and his conquest course
from Greece to India
to Babylon (334-323 BCE)

Alexander the
Great extended
the Macedonian
Empire to the areas
shown in red on
this map of the
ancient world.

ACROSS THE CENTURIES

To the land of Paeonia, legend continues, came Macedon, a son of Zeus, the king of the gods. The Macedonians were mountain people, fierce hunters and fighters, and said to be boisterous drinkers and dancers. The first known king of Macedonia was Caranus (also called Charon), who ruled from 808 to 778 BCE and established a kingdom that lasted for 400 years. The Macedonian kingdom expanded during the years that followed, from the reign of Caranus through 21 more kings, reaching its peak during the reign of Alexander the Great. Born in 356 BCE, Alexander inherited his throne at the age of 20, in 336 BCE, from his father, Philip II. He went on to extend the empire from Macedonia eastward and southward, from Greece to Egypt, and through Persia to northwestern India.

Alexander's early and sudden death in 323 BCE left the Macedonian Empire without a strong leader, and it fell into political and military disarray as rival leaders competed for power. Over the next 150 years, the Roman Empire waged war three times against the Macedonians, who were being fragmented and weakened. In 168 BCE, the Romans decisively defeated the last Macedonian king, Perseus, and took dominion over Macedonia.

Legend says that Alexander's beloved horse, Bucephalus, was originally a gift to his father, Philip II. When no one could tame the horse, 12-year-old Alexander took up the challenge. His father was angry at this display of pride and considered it an insult to the warriors who had already tried and failed to ride the horse. He told his son that if

he failed he would have to pay the price of the horse, a large amount of money that Alexander would have had difficulty raising. However, Alexander had noticed that when others tried to ride Bucephalus, the horse seemed to be afraid of his shadow, so he took the horse out into sunlight with his shadow behind him, whispered soothingly in his ear, and

Bucephalus is featured prominently in the huge statue of Alexander that was built in Skopje's central square in 2011.

peaceably mounted him. When he rode him past his father and dismounted, his father wept tears of joy and said, according to the writer Plutarch, "O my son, look thee out a kingdom equal to and worthy of thyself, for Macedonia is too little for thee."

Bucephalus and Alexander rode in hundreds of battles and over thousands of miles, partners in every battle Alexander fought in Greece and Asia. When the horse died of wounds received during a battle in India in 326 BCE, Alexander held a grand funeral and named a city in his honor.

Rome was determined that the Macedonian Empire would not rise again and to that end divided it into four autonomous regions. Each region was free to determine its own course, electing a magistrate and passing laws. Significantly, though, the regions could not trade or enter into alliances with each other,

Rendered in marble, King Samuel sits on his throne in Skopje.

thus assuring Rome that they would neither cooperate in any uprisings or unite into one nation.

Throughout the 800 years that followed, Rome expanded its empire throughout Europe and Asia. As a crossroads of trading routes, Macedonia was crucial to the empire, and towns, roads, and Christianity stabilized the region.

For nearly 100 years beginning in the mid-fifth century CE, Huns, Goths, and Avars laid waste to the Roman cities of Macedonia. What they did not ruin, an earthquake in 518 CE destroyed. The people of Macedonia downsized once more, forming small mountain communities centered on their churches. Their former international trading economy was reduced to subsistence farming.

Roving Slavic tribes moved into the vacuum created by the defeat of the Romans and the loose authority of the Bulgarians who had nominal rule. Taking advantage of the disunity in the region, the Slavs settled in the northern reaches of Macedonia. Over the next 300 years, they took Macedonia as their homeland, intermarrying and converting to Christianity, but preserving their own language. In 976, they proclaimed one of their own as king of Bulgaria. King Samuel (also called Czar Samuil) ruled until 1014, during which time the new kingdom developed its own church and a written language in which to conduct services.

The reign of King Samuel was not peaceful. The Bulgarians gave only a half-hearted effort to retaining their rule, besieged in their own land by the ascending forces of the Byzantine Empire, to which they finally fell. The conquering Byzantines were more engaged, however, and warred ceaselessly against the Bulgarian kingdom Samuel had based in what is today North Macedonia. When they finally defeated King Samuel's troops in 1014, they took the added precaution of blinding his surviving 15,000 soldiers, leaving only one eye for 100 men so they could find their way home. The march home took over two months. When King Samuel caught sight of his blinded and battered army staggering toward him, he suffered a heart attack and died days later.

The Byzantines ruled Macedonia until the beginning of the 14th century, when the Ottoman Empire defeated them throughout their lands. During this time, Macedonia played reluctant host to Norman raiders and Christian crusaders, as well as paying taxes and serving in the armies of the Byzantine conquerors.

OTTOMAN RULE

By 1394, Ottoman control of Macedonia was complete and would remain absolute for the next 500 years. In Macedonia, as elsewhere in the Balkan lands, uprisings occurred, but they were never long-lasting or successful, and they were savagely put down. The Turks reestablished towns and trade and introduced Islam and its legal system, as well as Turkish architecture and art. Through Turkish forbearance and Macedonian persistence, however, Macedonian culture maintained its hold on its people through the unifying influences of Christianity and language.

TOWARD A NATIONAL CONSCIOUSNESS

The 19th century was a time of great ethnic and nationalistic fervor in Macedonia. Macedonia's neighbors, Greece, Bulgaria, and Serbia, newly liberated from the Turks, turned their attentions and aspirations toward Macedonia. They opened schools, promoted their languages and religions, and influenced the Turks in developing roads and railway routes to their countries. The Greeks and Bulgarians also sent roving bands of guerrillas to use force and fear to convince the Macedonians to reconsider their national loyalty and ethnic identity.

With the Turks still in control of their country and their neighbors beating on the doors, Macedonians in the second half of the 19th century began to organize.

The first stage of organization was a development of national consciousness. To that end, education and literature flourished, and the people became literate and aware of their own identity. Soon, revolutionary leaders emerged, and uprisings against the Turks in 1876 and 1878, though unsuccessful in their aim, raised the desire for national independence and solidified the movement. In 1893, the Internal Macedonian Revolutionary Organization (IMRO) emerged with Gotse Delchev as its leader and "Macedonia for the Macedonians" as its slogan. On August 2, 1903, the IMRO declared Macedonian independence in what came to be called the Ilinden Uprising. The Turks reacted immediately and brutally, suppressing the revolt, but the Macedonians had grabbed international attention. Though the revolt was unsuccessful, Macedonians look to the date of the declaration, August 2, 1903, as the symbolic beginning of their nation, and it is celebrated as a national holiday.

MACEDONIA NO MORE

International intervention resulted in the division of Macedonia after the Ottoman Empire relinquished control. The Turks were out, but the neighbors were in. The largest part, the Aegean region, went to Greece, which called it Northern Greece. The Pirin region in the east went to Bulgaria, which abolished the Macedonian name. The Vardar region to the north went to Serbia, and it was renamed Southern Serbia. The leaders of Greece and Serbia agreed on a border—only Serbs lived to the north of the border, only Greeks to the south, and Macedonians theoretically no longer existed. All three former neighbors imposed their identity on the Macedonians, either denying their ethnicity entirely or treating them as inferior in an attempt to encourage their assimilation. Greece was particularly intent on obliterating all signs of Macedonian history by changing names of villages, rivers, mountains, and other geographical locations. Macedonians were forced to renounce their names in favor of Greek-sounding names and were forbidden to speak their own language.

THE 1900s

The Macedonian parcels of land continued to be batted about throughout the first half of the 20th century. During World War I (1914—1918), Bulgaria occupied the Vardar region that had been Serbia's, but when the war ended with Bulgaria on the losing side, Serbia got it back. The powers that carved Europe into new nations at the Paris Peace Conference in 1918 ignored Macedonian pleas for a united and independent nation. Instead, they made Vardar Macedonia a part

BALKANIZE: THE EVOLUTION OF A WORD

When Yugoslavia was created after World War I from the territories inhabited by various Balkan peoples, a new verb was created as well: "balkanize." The word means "to divide or break up a region or body into smaller, mutually hostile states or groups." "Balkanization" is the noun form of the word. When referring to a multiethnic nation, it typically means the dividing into smaller, ethnically homogenous entities.

The term balkanization is today used to explain the disintegration of some multiethnic states and their decline into dictatorship, ethnic cleansing, and civil war. It is sometimes considered a derogatory word.

of the newly proclaimed Kingdom of the Serbs, Croats, and Slovenes, which became Yugoslavia in 1929.

Between the two world wars, Macedonians worked to unite their nation once again, but to no avail. The governments that controlled them were very strong and oppressive, and Macedonian nationalism came at a high price to its participants. However, literary activity flourished, and in Vienna, Austria, expatriates began to organize for the day when they could go home to a free and united Macedonia.

When World War II (1939–1945) broke out, Bulgaria once again took over all of the former Macedonia, including the Vardar and Aegean regions. Allied with the Nazis, they collaborated in sending the Jews of the region to their deaths. By 1943, though, the Macedonian communists were gaining strength and sympathy due to their desire to throw the Bulgarians out. They formed the Communist Party of Macedonia, established an army, and set up local and national liberation councils. When, as in World War I, it became clear that Bulgaria had chosen the losing side, they were driven out of the lands they occupied.

In April 1945, the Macedonian resistance founded the first Macedonian government, a free state within the Yugoslav Federation. Macedonians from all three parts of the divided country celebrated, although only the Vardar lands were affected. The free state was called the People's Republic of Macedonia. In 1963, when Yugoslavia officially changed its name to the Socialist Federal

Kiro Gligorov
(1917-2012) was
the first president
of the independent
Republic of
Macedonia, serving
from 1991 to 1999.

Republic of Yugoslavia, Macedonia was also renamed, becoming the Socialist Republic of Macedonia.

INDEPENDENCE

In 1991, the Federation of Yugoslavia began to dissolve during the general collapse of communism in Europe. Slovenia, Croatia, and Bosnia declared their independence. On September 8, Macedonians voted to declare their independence as well and proclaimed themselves the independent Republic of Macedonia. Kiro Gligorov was elected the first president. In 1993, Macedonia was admitted to the United Nations (UN).

A ROCKY ROAD

The years since independence have been challenging. Initially, Greece's hostility toward the new country was very damaging. It imposed a trade embargo and pressured other European countries not to do business with Macedonia. Furthermore, despite the constitution's declaration of ethnic equality, some of Macedonia's ethnic minorities, in particular the Albanians, felt that they were being unfairly represented.

Things came to a head in 2001 when the Albanian National Liberation Army (NLA) attacked Macedonian security forces near the Kosovo border. Though the NLA stated it was merely fighting for greater rights for Albanians, some observers suspected that the group's true goal was secession of Albanian-majority areas from the republic.

The hostilities in Macedonia lasted almost 10 months, with dozens of deaths on both sides, before ending with the Ohrid Framework Agreement in August 2001. The peace treaty, negotiated by US and European diplomats, created a framework for the reform of minority political and cultural rights within Macedonia. It remains the principal guide for maintaining ethnic peace in North Macedonia today.

The country encountered yet more bumps on its way to stability. A political scandal in 2014 led to public demonstrations and two years of crisis

For much of the 20th century, what is today's North Macedonia was part of the country of Yugoslavia. It began after World War I as the Kingdom of the Serbs, Croats, and Slovenes. Macedonia had, by that time, already been incorporated into Serbia. In 1929, it took the name Kingdom of Yugoslavia.

In 1941, during World War II, Yugoslavia tried to remain neutral, but it was invaded by German, Italian, Hungarian, and Bulgarian forces (otherwise known as some of the Axis forces). After the war, Yugoslavia was re-created as a socialist federation made up of six constituent republics: Bosnia-Herzegovina, Croatia, Macedonia, Montenegro, Serbia, and Slovenia. Serbia contained two autonomous provinces, Vojvodina and Kosovo. The capital was Belgrade, which today is the capital of Serbia.

Shown here is the former Yugoslavia.

The president of this new iteration of Yugoslavia, beginning in 1953, was Josip Broz, known as Tito. During World War II, he had led the Yugoslav guerrilla movement, the Partisans, which were a Yugoslav communist resistance group fighting the Axis forces. Tito remained Yugoslavia's president (later "president for life") until his death in 1980. Although he was a dictator, he allowed broad freedoms in science, art, and culture that were inconceivable in the Soviet Union and the Eastern European countries of the Soviet bloc.

Yugoslavia would not last long without Tito. By 1991, the Socialist Federal Republic of Yugoslavia had broken apart. A third, smaller iteration of a nation bearing the name Yugoslavia was made up of only Serbia and Montenegro. It existed from 1992 to 2003.

When Macedonia declared its independence in 1991, Greece, its neighbor to the south, was immediately hostile to the name of the new country. The name Macedonia is also attached to three northern provinces in Greece, including Central Macedonia, the largest and second most populous province. These provinces encompass the southern part of the geographical region of Macedonia.

Between the newly independent nation that was once a part of Yugoslavia, the Greek provinces, and the historical geographic region, there were altogether too many Macedonias competing for the same name. Meanwhile, both Greece and the Republic of Macedonia struggled to assert historical ownership of the name, both reaching back to ancient times to lobby for their position.

The dispute escalated, and international mediators attempted to intervene. The United Nations oversaw negotiations, agreeing to accept any mutually agreed upon solution. As the dispute lingered, the Republic of Macedonia found itself forced into identifying as the "the Former Yugoslav Republic of Macedonia," or FYROM.

In 2018, the two nations reached an agreement whereby the Republic of Macedonia would become the Republic of North Macedonia. The question was put to voters in a referendum. A majority supported the change, though voter turnout was very low. The country changed its name officially on January 11, 2019. Doing so opened the door for North Macedonia to apply for membership in both the European Union and NATO, a move that had been blocked by Greece prior to the name change.

in the government. The ethnic Albanian problem rose up again in 2017 when ethnic Slav Macedonian nationalists violently stormed the North Macedonian parliament in protest over the election of Talat Xhaferi as president of the legislature—the first ethnic Albanian to hold the post. The incident came to be called "Bloody Thursday," as Zoran Zaev, leader of the Social Democrats and soon-to-be prime minister, was himself bloodied by the attack.

INTERNET LINKS

https://www.ancient.eu/macedon
The Ancient History Encyclopedia entry on Macedon includes a section on Alexander the Great.

https://www.bbc.com/news/world-europe-17553072
The BBC offers a timeline of key events in the history of North Macedonia, beginning in 1913.

https://history.state.gov/milestones/1989-1992/breakup-yugoslavia
The US State Department Office of the Historian details the breakup of Yugoslavia.

https://www.lonelyplanet.com/north-macedonia/background/ history/a/nar/8efe5a07-607f-4d45-80dd-01ab3a047f4d/360131
Lonely Planet provides a good overview of North Macedonia's history.

https://www.nytimes.com/2017/04/27/world/europe/macedonia -parliament-attacked-nationalists.html?_r=0
This *New York Times* article about the nationalist attack on parliament in 2017 includes a video and numerous photos of the mayhem.

GOVERNMENT

ВЛАДА НА РЕПУБЛИКА МАКЕДОНИЈА

The red and yellow flag of North Macedonia flies
outside the Government Building in Skopje.

3

THE REPUBLIC OF NORTH Macedonia is a parliamentary republic with a multiparty political system. It is governed by a president, a prime minister, and a parliament, or legislature. The judiciary, or court system, is an independent branch of the government. The country has experienced some rocky times in its newest incarnation as an independent nation, but it strives for democracy, freedom, and stability.

As Yugoslavia was disintegrating at the beginning of the 1990s, 95 percent of voting Macedonians approved the independence and sovereignty of the Republic of Macedonia on September 8, 1991. The new constitution declared the Republic of Macedonia a sovereign, independent, civil, and democratic state, and it recognized the complete equality of the Macedonians and all ethnic minorities. On April 8, 1993, the Republic of Macedonia was unanimously and with acclamation admitted to the United Nations as its 181st member.

THE PRESPA AGREEMENT

Greece, the country's neighbor to the south, which was never part of Yugoslavia, was not pleased with the name of the new republic. The name Macedonia also belongs to the northernmost region in Greece, and the

The North Macedonian flag features a yellow, eight-rayed sunburst against a red background. The republic's first flag, adopted in 1992, depicted the so-called Vergina Sun, a 16-rayed sunburst design dating from ancient Macedon. However, Greece objected, as it considers the Vergina Sun to be a Greek symbol. Greece imposed an economic embargo to force then-Macedonia to replace the design, which it did in 1995.

Република Македонија

РЕПУБЛИКА СЕВЕРНА МАКЕДОНИЈ

REPUBLIC OF NORTH MACEDONI

Workers replace a sign with the country's new name at the border between North Macedonia and Greece near Gevgelija on February 13, 2019.

government of Greece believed the new Republic of Macedonia was usurping the name. In June 2018, after 27 years of disputes and negotiations, the two countries settled their differences by signing the Prespa Agreement. (The name reflects the site of the signing ceremonies on the banks of Lake Prespa.) The accord stipulated that the Republic of Macedonia would change its name to the Republic of North Macedonia, and that Greece would accept it and eliminate all prior objections.

In a September 2018 referendum, the people of Macedonia voiced approval of the Prespa Agreement by a 91 percent majority. However, the voter turnout was only 37 percent, below the 50 percent required. This was not due to a lack of interest on the part of Macedonian voters. Rather, the Internal Macedonian Revolutionary Organization—Democratic Party for Macedonian Unity (VMRO-DPMNE), a political party including then-president Gjorge Ivanov, had urged people to boycott the vote. The VMRO-DPMNE is a center-right to right-wing nationalist, conservative party. In recent years, it has looked to Russia and taken an anti-Western, anti-NATO stance. Meanwhile, the opposition Social Democratic Union of Macedonia (SDSM), a center-left party, campaigned in favor of the referendum and the agreement.

With the referendum results thrown out for lack of sufficient voter participation, it was then left to the parliament to approve the agreement, which it did in November 2018. The name change took effect in January 2019.

THE CONSTITUTION

On November 17, 1991, then-Macedonia adopted the new Constitution of the Republic of Macedonia. The constitution guarantees the rule of law, a democratic political system, and individual rights. This constitution remains in place, along with the amendments added on January 11, 2019, regarding the country's name change.

The values the government and the people of North Macedonia aspire to are encoded in the constitution. Among these are the right to vote for all citizens over 18, the protection of property from unlawful seizure, the right to artistic and political expression, freedom to conduct and own businesses, political pluralism, free expression of national identity, and respect for international law. Basic freedoms and the rights of the individual are spelled out. For example:

- Article 9 states, "Citizens of the Republic of Macedonia are equal in their freedoms and rights, regardless of sex, race, color of skin, national and social origin, political and religious beliefs, property and social status. All citizens are equal before the Constitution and law."
- Article 10 asserts that the death penalty is illegal: "The human right to life is irrevocable. The death penalty shall not be imposed on any grounds whatsoever in the Republic of North Macedonia."
- Article 11 outlaws torture and forced labor.
- Article 19 guarantees the right to religious expression as well as the separation of church and state.
- Article 20 confers freedom of association and the establishment of political parties. However, this article does prohibit political

parties and other associations that are targeted at the violent destruction of the government or "at encouragement or incitement to military aggression or ethnic, racial or religious hatred or intolerance." Similarly, "military or paramilitary associations which do not belong to the Armed Forces of the Republic of Macedonia are prohibited."

GOVERNMENT STRUCTURE

As is typical in most parliamentary republics, the power of the president is fairly limited, and most executive power resides in the office of the prime minister and the council of ministers (the cabinet). In North Macedonia, the president, the prime minister, and the cabinet ministers are all granted immunity from prosecution by the constitution.

THE PRESIDENT   The president is the head of state. He or she is elected directly by an absolute majority vote of the people to a term of five years

Stevo Pendarovski of the Social Democratic Union of Macedonia (SDSM) declares his presidential election victory in Skopje on May 5, 2019.

and may serve two terms. If the first round of elections does not produce an absolute majority winner, then a run-off election follows. Voter turnout must be at least 40 percent for the election to be valid. In 2019, Stevo Pendarovski (b. 1963) became president. He is a member of the SDSM. The next election is set for 2024.

The president is the commander in chief of the armed forces. He or she appoints diplomatic ambassadors, proposes two judicial appointees, appoints three members of the Security Council, and grants decorations, honors, and pardons. The president also represents the republic at foreign events.

THE PRIME MINISTER The North Macedonian constitution describes the prime minister and the ministers of the cabinet together as "the Government." The prime minister is the head of government and holds the most executive power. The parliament elects the prime minister, who also leads the cabinet of ministers. He or she serves with no term limit. In May 2017, Zoran Zaev (b. 1974) of the SDSM became the prime minister. Prior to that, he had been the mayor of Strumica, a large city in eastern North Macedonia.

Prime Minister Zoran Zaev appears before the media at the EU Commission headquarters in Brussels, Belgium.

The prime minister chooses the cabinet ministers, who are then approved by parliament.

THE ASSEMBLY   The legislative branch of the government, also called the parliament, is the unicameral, or one-house, legislative body called the Assembly (or Sobranie). It's composed of 120 directly elected representatives of the people who serve four-year terms. Critical to the election of the Assembly is the constitutionally guaranteed right of people to form political parties.

The duties of the Assembly include adopting and interpreting laws, adopting a budget and spending the money collected, ratifying international agreements, declaring war and peace, electing and dismissing judges and holders of other offices, and electing the government of the Republic of North Macedonia. Any member of the Assembly can propose a law. In addition, a law can be introduced by a petition signed by 10,000 voters. Laws are passed by a simple majority of the representatives. The president of the republic can veto the law, which can be returned for another vote. If the law then passes by a margin of two-thirds, the president is required to sign it into law.

The parliament is headed by a president elected by 61 or more of the assembly members for a term of four years. The parliamentary president's duties are to run the governmental sessions and see that the rules of parliamentary procedure are followed. If the president of the republic is unable to govern, the president of the parliament takes over that office.

THE JUDICIARY   Judges are elected to unrestricted terms of office by the parliament. North Macedonia has 27 regular courts, 4 courts of appeal, and a supreme court. The Supreme Court has 22 judges. Additionally, there is the Constitutional Court, with 9 judges, which is charged with ensuring that there is no conflict of interest or abuse of power among the three branches of the government. The judges of the Constitutional Court

Government buildings stand on the Vardar River in Skopje, near the famed Art Bridge, which features statues of noted Macedonian artists and musicians.

serve for nine non-renewable years. The constitution of North Macedonia specifically prohibits the creation of any emergency or other special court. This prohibition reflects the country's history as part of Yugoslavia, where secret, military, or special government courts operated as part of a system of government oppression.

LOCAL GOVERNMENT

Local governments are elected by citizens of municipalities. These governments can collect taxes to finance the municipality, though the republic also provides funds. Citizens participate in their local governments both directly and through their elected representatives. The level of participation often depends on the size of the municipality, with people in villages and smaller towns being more directly involved. Governmental issues such as urban planning, communal activities, sports, childcare, preschool education, primary education, and basic health care are usually decided at the local level.

AN ETHNIC DILEMMA

Ethnic Macedonians and ethnic Albanians in the Republic of North Macedonia have distinctly different but equally ethnocentric views of the causes and course of the armed conflict that raged between them in 2001. These attitudes have impeded efforts to diminish animosities and have the potential for fueling further violence.

The fighting between armed Albanians and Macedonian security forces in 2001 ended in August of that year when they signed the Ohrid Framework Agreement. In September, the voters passed amendments to the constitution, giving greater recognition to the Albanian language and greater power to local Albanian minorities. Since then, many of North Macedonia's political leaders have vowed to develop cooperation between the two ethnic communities. A daunting challenge facing the country is to find a way to promote cooperation at the social level, as well as the political, between groups that have been separated by language, religion, and culture.

In late 2014, when the country was still known as Macedonia, a government scandal provoked public protests and threw the nation into a political crisis that would continue for two years. At the time, the VMRO-DPMNE was the party in power, and it had held the majority in government for eight years. Nikola Gruevski (b. 1970) was the prime minister, and Gjorge Ivanov (b. 1960) was the president. The party's popularity was declining, however, amid accusations of corruption and high levels of unemployment.

In the lead-up to the 2014 elections, Zoran Zaev, then the leader of the opposition SDSM party, charged the incumbent party officials with election fraud. The VMRO-DPMNE, for its part, charged Zaev with conspiracy to overthrow the government. Zaev went on to reveal that Prime Minister Gruevski, along with the country's security and counterintelligence agency, the UBK, had allegedly wiretapped around 20,000 Macedonian citizens, including opposition politicians and journalists. Zaev also charged that Gruevski had been involved with covering up a political murder. As proof, Zaev released around 670,000 wiretapped recordings of phone conversations.

In addition, an unnamed whistle-blower released taped conversations between Gruevski and other officials, revealing discussions about illegal interventions in elections and judicial affairs, and against journalists and opposition politicians.

The allegations prompted a series of public protests demanding the resignation of Gruevski, which continued into 2015. In May of that year, 30,000 to 50,000 anti-government protesters rallied in Skopje. Pro-government counter-

Protesters demonstrate in Skopje against Prime Minister Nikola Gruevski in May 2015.

protesters rallied the following day. Although several other high-ranking officials resigned, Gruevski refused to step down. At that point, the EU stepped in to negotiate a settlement. The resulting Przino Agreement of July 2015 called for Gruevski's early resignation and scheduled an early general election for June 2016.

Although Gruevski eventually resigned in 2016, investigations into his illegal activities continued. President Ivanov halted judicial inquiries into the wiretap scandal, granting amnesty to those involved—a move which spurred more protests. Those demonstrations, which continued from April to June 2016, came to be called the "Colorful Revolution," as some protesters threw paintballs at government buildings. Gruevski was eventually found guilty on other corruption charges. In May 2018, he was sentenced to two years in prison. However, he then fled to Hungary, with the covert help of the Hungarian government, where he remains a fugitive.

Meanwhile, the election of 2016 brought Zaev's SDSM party into power, and in 2017, Zaev himself became the prime minister. In 2019, at the end of President Ivanov's term, a new president was elected, Stevo Pendarovski.

INTERNET LINKS

https://freedomhouse.org/report/freedom-world/2019/ north-macedonia
Freedom House reports annually on the country's state of freedom and democracy.

https://www.globalsecurity.org/military/world/europe/ mk-ohrid.htm
This site provides an in-depth look at the Ohrid Agreement of 2001.

https://www.sobranie.mk/the-constitution-of-the-republic-of -macedonia-ns_article-constitution-of-the-republic-of-north -macedonia.nspx
The official site of the Assembly of the Republic of North Macedonia provides an English-language version of the constitution.

ECONOMY

A North Macedonian 5-denar coin showing a lynx lies on a scattering of denar banknotes.

4

S INCE 1991, WHEN NORTH Macedonia became an independent nation called Macedonia, it has made progress in the economic transition to a thriving market economy. At first, Macedonia's economy was part of the economy of a now-collapsed union. The newly free nation therefore had a lot of work to do.

As a Yugoslav republic, Macedonia had a centrally planned economy, with state ownership of property and industry. It was the poorest and least economically developed republic in Yugoslavia. The Yugoslav plan had assigned to Macedonia the role of building and running plants for heavy industry, which have since been vacated with the loss of their partners in the former Yugoslav republics.

The years that followed further weakened Macedonia's economy. No longer did it receive aid from a central government, trade was restricted by an embargo imposed on Serbia, Greece imposed an embargo on Macedonia, Albania's even weaker economy left it unsuitable as a trading partner, and Bulgaria nursed bad feelings toward the new republic, making it disinclined to trade with Macedonia. War conditions in Kosovo through 2001 limited international investment and participation in Macedonia as well.

In the 21st century, however, things began to look up. Much of the country's industry has been transferred to private ownership. The government has invested in roads, airports, railways, and hydroelectric

The North Macedonian government counts a labor force of about 950,800 workers, but about 22.4 percent of them are unemployed. Approximately 16.2 percent work in agriculture, 29.2 percent work in industry, and 54.5 percent have jobs in the service sector.

A centrally
planned economy
is one in which
the government
controls and
regulates
production,
distribution, and
prices. Such
economies usually
involve state-
owned enterprises.
Communism
is based on a
centrally planned
economy.

A market economy
is one in which
production
and prices are
determined by
competition
between privately
owned businesses.
Capitalism is
based on a market
economy.

plants. Trade prospects with Bulgaria, Greece, Serbia, and Albania have improved since the cessation of hostilities and lifting of embargoes.

The political crises of 2014 to 2018 slowed economic progress, but opportunities exist for improvement. Resolution of the name dispute with Greece should open new markets. A change of government brings new hope as well. The SDSM's reform agenda focuses on economic growth, job creation, fair taxation, support to small and medium enterprises, and reform of social protections for the most vulnerable.

Foreign investment is expected to increase with political stability. In 2018, following the agreement with Greece, North Macedonia received $700 million in foreign investment—double the average rate of the previous five years. This accounted for 5.9 percent of the country's gross domestic product (GDP). North Macedonians think joining NATO could boost that investment even more.

INDUSTRY AND ENERGY

Today, the country's main industries include the production of automotive parts, textiles, iron, steel, chemicals, cement, and pharmaceuticals. Because its industry is primarily low-tech while requiring comparatively high-cost labor, it is at a disadvantage compared with countries like China and India.

In terms of energy, North Macedonia relies primarily on fossil fuels for its electrical needs. The country derives about 60 percent of its electricity from fossil fuel power plants and about 37 percent of its power from hydroelectric plants. The existing thermal power plants are largely obsolete and in need of modernization. There are no nuclear energy plants in North Macedonia. A wind power farm exists in the southern part of the country, and there are plans to increase its capacity.

Although it produces most of its own electricity, the country still needs to import all of its fuels to meet its total domestic requirements. A pipeline that brought oil from the Greek port city of Thessaloniki to the country's only refinery, OKTA, was shut down in 2013 by its owner Hellenic Petroleum. However, in 2019, talks were on to reopen the line and have it serve as a hub for the greater Balkan region. North Macedonia's name change was one of

> **WHAT IS GDP?**

Gross domestic product (GDP) is a measure of a country's total production. The number reflects the total value of goods and services produced over one year. Economists use it to determine whether a country's economy is growing or contracting. Growth is good, while a falling GDP means trouble. Dividing the GDP by the number of people in the country determines the GDP per capita (per person). This number provides an indication of a country's average standard of living—the higher the better.

In 2017, the GDP per capita in then-Macedonia was $14,900. That figure ranked Macedonia at number 113 out of 228 countries listed by the CIA World Factbook. For comparison, the United States that year was number 19, with a GDP per capita of $59,800. Serbia was about the same as Macedonia, with a GDP per capita of $15,100. Albania was lower, with $12,500, and Bulgaria was considerably higher, with $21,800. Macedonia's neighbor to the south, Greece, was higher still, with $27,800.

several factors spurring talks of reopening the line. In addition, a natural gas pipeline brings Russian gas from the Bulgarian border to Skopje. The gas distribution network is still under development.

Macedonia once supplied much of Yugoslavia with hydroelectric power, but today, it needs to construct more plants to provide enough for its own use. More capacity will be required to support the growth of the country's industrial sector. The North Macedonian government hopes that increased international aid and investment to rebuild its hydroelectric industry will also result in industrial partnerships. North Macedonia adopted a new energy law in 2018, aligning its energy legislation with that of the EU.

AGRICULTURE

In 2018, exports of agriculture and food products made up about 10 percent of North Macedonia's total exports. The country's warm climate and abundant water resources make it suitable for growing a wide variety of crops. Tomatoes, peppers, corn, grapes, rice, tobacco, and wheat thrive on small family farms reclaimed from the large communist-owned collectives. Dairy farming is also important, as is livestock, though generally for home consumption rather than export. The agricultural strengths of Macedonia are reflected in its cuisine, where lamb and beef, tomatoes and peppers, and honey-sweetened desserts are popular.

Among its agricultural products, tobacco remains one of North Macedonia's main exports. Tobacco sheds with their drying racks are scattered throughout the countryside.

Despite the importance of agriculture, farm productivity is low, with limited use of technology and too many workers using inefficient methods. A lack of large-scale refrigeration and shipping systems means the agricultural sector can supply only what is in season. The grape industry is beginning to overcome some of these drawbacks as wineries develop near vineyards. Wine is becoming a successful and growing North Macedonian industry and export.

Farming in North Macedonia is very labor intensive. On many farms, animals rather than machines still pull the plows and the market wagons. Farming on

Tobacco grows under the hot sun in the rich soil of a mountain valley.

the terraced lands of the mountains can be a community project, as people gather to plant or harvest one farm at a time until all the farms in the area are finished. This communal activity is not so much a reflection of a communist past, but rather of a much older tradition. During Macedonia's centuries of invasions, farmers built their houses in small village clusters as protection from marauders. Each morning, they left to work their outlying fields. Though the fields were family-owned, the farmers had a sense of community that still serves them well and prevented the isolation experienced by farmers and their families in other lands.

MINERALS

Besides iron and zinc, which it exports, North Macedonia also produces copper, gold, silver, manganese, tungsten, lead, and nickel. These resources are running low, however, and will have to be imported if their use is to continue. Macedonia still has large amounts of materials used in the building industry: marble, granite, gypsum, siliceous and quartz sands, and lignite.

INTERNET LINKS

https://www.export.gov/article?id=North-Macedonia-Energy
This site provides information about energy sources in North Macedonia.

https://www.worldbank.org/en/country/northmacedonia
The World Bank gives an overview of North Macedonia's economy.

ENVIRONMENT

A plume of air pollutants rises against a Skopje sunrise.

LIKE ANY COUNTRY, NORTH Macedonia has environmental problems. Air and water pollution are particular concerns, especially around Skopje. Metallurgical plants in the industrial regions pollute the air, and insufficient, or even a complete lack of, sewage treatment contaminates the waters. Chemical factories, leather production, food production, and metallurgic industries are all guilty of severe water pollution.

In the winter months, atmospheric conditions press colder, heavier air down into the Skopje valley, and a haze settles over the city. The smog is an unhealthy mix of ash and chemicals. A large number of people heat their homes with wood, and the smoke in the winter contributes to the air pollution. On the streets, a high percentage of vehicles are old and unregulated, and their emissions contribute as well. Outdated, coal-fired power plants add to the smog.

In agricultural areas, farmers dump untreated livestock waste straight into the rivers, as do slaughterhouses and other food-based industries. Even Lake Ohrid, which is internationally protected, suffers from euthrophication due to the inflow of wastewater. Euthrophication is an excess of nutrients that causes a dense growth of plant life. This

5

In 2018, the United Nations Environment Programme named Skopje "Europe's most polluted capital." The report focused on the North Macedonian city's poor air quality.

leads to a lowered oxygen level in the water, which kills off animal life. Harmful algae blooms, dead zones, and fish kills are often the result in bodies of water that exhibit this unhealthy condition.

In order to be accepted into the European Union, North Macedonia must demonstrate progress in several areas of environmental protection. A 2019 EU report found that the country had made "limited progress" in achieving its goals. North Macedonia was said to be lagging in its enforcement and implementation of environmental laws.

LAKE OHRID: AN INTERNATIONAL ISSUE

Lake Ohrid—which spans both Albania and North Macedonia—contains snails, crabs, and flatworms that have evolved and persisted nowhere else on Earth. Seventeen types of fish and nearly 200 other species of animals are indigenous to the lake. Today, this collection of rare marine life, having survived millions of years, is threatened by extinction.

Green algae blooms under the water and on the rocks in Lake Ohrid.

In Lake Ohrid, the Ohrid trout barely survives in an environment of overfishing and pollution. Scientists fear that it might be too late, even with a ban on fishing, to save the ancient species. Ohrid trout is a celebrated local dish in North Macedonia. Hatcheries around the lake have supported its preservation and consumption, but still the population of the 25-pound (11-kilogram) fish has continued to drop. Hatchery workers have been unable to collect more than half the eggs needed to keep the trout population at its current level.

In 1996, the Lake Ohrid Conservation Project was formed to preserve the biodiversity of the 19-mile- (30 km) long lake. The study concluded that overfishing, both legal and illegal, from North Macedonia and Albania needed to be better managed. With commercial fishing removing about 80 tons (73 metric tons) of trout a year and illegal fishing taking untold numbers of fish, the Macedonian government imposed a ban on trout fishing from 2004 to 2014. Albania did not follow suit.

The tourism industry relies on the Ohrid trout to attract international fishermen, who are drawn to Lake Ohrid by the possibility of catching a 25-pound fish. Families in both countries have supported themselves by fishing in Lake Ohrid. With few opportunities for employment in both countries, fishing bans are not popular.

The difficulty of solving the problems of overfishing and pollution in Lake Ohrid is made more complex by the fact that the lake belongs to two countries. Isolated from each other for many years, North Macedonia and Albania have not had a history of cooperation or sharing information. Still, the lake is important to both countries, and the Lake Ohrid Conservation Project brought the two countries together to preserve the lake for their mutual benefit. As a start, they agreed that Lake Ohrid and its watershed constitute one ecosystem, and that all governments in the watershed must share in its management.

For North Macedonia, the town of Ohrid and the surrounding region are a popular tourist area and a UNESCO World Heritage site. When UNESCO expressed grave concerns in 2017 about environmental deterioration of the region, it was a heads-up alert for the country. However, at the time, Macedonia was still climbing out of its political crisis and perhaps had limited resources to focus on the issue. Among UNESCO's concerns about Ohrid were illegal

THE ENVIRONMENTAL LEGACY OF WAR

In 2001, the warring factions of ethnic Albanians (NLA) and Macedonian government forces signed a peace accord brokered by NATO. Under that agreement, the NATO Task Force Harvest destroyed weapons turned over by the NLA amounting to 1,054 land mines and grenades and 354 other explosive devices. Still, people continued to die from unexploded ordnance (UXOs) and land mines as they returned to villages that had been bombarded by Macedonian security forces.

NATO and other international organizations provided assistance to Macedonia to demine roads and to locate UXOs so that people could return to their homes. With the assistance of the International Trust Fund for Demining and Mine Victims Assistance (ITF), they cleared 879 houses, 1,394 other buildings, and 11.7 miles (18.8 km) of railway and roads in the last three months of 2001. The clearance resulted in the destruction of 153 UXOs and 4 mines. By 2006, Macedonia had fulfilled its obligations and was theoretically mine-free. UXOs from earlier wars may remain, however. Such unwanted leftovers from long-ago wars can be particularly dangerous during natural disasters and fires. In 2019, for example, firefighters were prevented from fully controlling a spate of forest fires in several regions of North Macedonia, including Galicica National Park, because of the possibility of UXOs dating from World War I.

Meanwhile, the Macedonian Red Cross developed a mine/UXO awareness program to help people recognize and avoid the dangers that persisted after the end of the conflict, especially in the north and northwest parts of the country. The danger was acute as farmers returned to their fields in the spring of 2002 to plow and sow. International relief groups held information sessions in the villages, sometimes visiting homes of people who did not attend. Leaflets and posters were distributed to villagers. One of the leaflets was aimed at children and featured a cartoon character based on the famous Macedonian Shara dog, familiar to all Macedonian children.

However, Lake Ohrid harbored dangers of its own in the form of underwater UXOs. Since 2006, the ITF has been supporting North Macedonia in the challenging problem of underwater UXO contamination of Lake Ohrid. ITF supported three underwater UXO clearance phases of Lake Ohrid, allowing 612,470 square feet (56,900 square meters) of lake bottom to be cleared. Altogether, over 6,600 UXOs have been safely removed and destroyed.

construction, traffic, tourism development, overfishing, sewage, solid waste disposal, invasive species, and insufficient environmental management.

In 2019, when UNESCO warned that it was considering reclassifying the site as "endangered," North Macedonia knew it had to act fast, but political bickering quickly ensued as the VMRO-DPMNE and SDSM parties blamed each other for the problems. UNESCO's report presented 19 requirements to be addressed no later than February 2020.

At the same time, UNESCO extended the scope of the protected site to include the Albanian part of the lake as well. The World Heritage site now includes the entire lake and the surrounding towns of Ohrid and Struga in North Macedonia, and Pogradec in Albania.

INTERNET LINKS

https://www.balcanicaucaso.org/eng/Areas/North-Macedonia/Ohrid-and-its-lake-a-UNESCO-heritage-in-danger-196684
This article discusses UNESCO's concerns about its World Heritage site in the Lake Ohrid region.

https://pulitzercenter.org/reporting/ancient-valleys-macedonia-pall-air-pollution
"In the Ancient Valleys of Macedonia, a Pall of Air Pollution" is an in-depth story with many photos and videos.

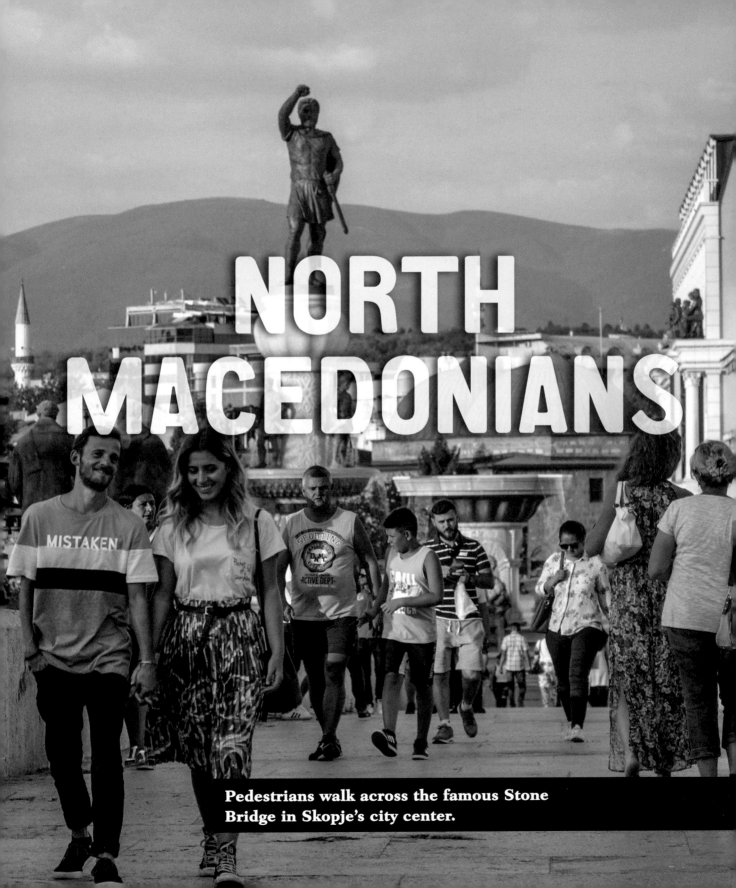

NORTH MACEDONIANS

Pedestrians walk across the famous Stone Bridge in Skopje's city center.

6

D EFINING A PEOPLE CAN BE
difficult. People can be described by
nationality, ethnicity, race, language,
and religion. North Macedonia and its
neighboring Balkan countries have always
been multiethnic and multilingual. Perhaps
it was inevitable, then, that the ethnicity
of the North Macedonian people would be
a subject of long-standing controversy.

North Macedonia is a political designation. It's the name of the nation,
and its citizens are called North Macedonians. However, when speaking
of ethnicity, "Macedonian" is the term, as ethnicity is not bound by
national borders. Indeed, some ethnic Albanians and ethnic Bulgarians
are North Macedonians, by virtue of shifting boundaries over the course of
history. However, some people dispute the very concept of a Macedonian
ethnicity, saying such a group has never existed. Rather, they assert that
Macedonians are a South Slavic ethnic group native to the geographical
region of Macedonia. As might be expected, some Macedonians take
umbrage at being labeled Slavs.

So, just who are the North Macedonians? Serbs have claimed them as
Serbian because they have similar folk customs. Bulgaria has claimed them
as Bulgarian because the Macedonian language is similar to Bulgarian.
Greece has called them Macedonian Greeks because there have been
Slavic-speaking Greeks in the area since Alexander the Great.

Today's 2,119,000 North Macedonians are still divided in opinion and
in ethnicity. Who can claim Macedonian ethnic identity is a matter of

Having gone without
an official census
since 2002 because
of the failed
2011 census,
North Macedonia
announced in May
2019 its intent to
conduct a census
in April 2020. The
count will collect
data on geographical
and demographical
features, the
economy, education,
migration, ethnicity,
and religion. The
effort was expected
to take about
6,000 workers at
a cost of around
$9.4 million.

Performers dressed in traditional costumes participate in the Skopje International Festival of Music and Dance in 2018.

some dispute. The claims are often based on history going back thousands of years, their accounts sometimes grounded in legend or religious documents and beliefs. Setting aside the question of who has the most right to call themselves Macedonian, several ethnic groups have a prominent presence in North Macedonia—Macedonians, Albanians, Turks, Vlachs, and Roma.

Under communist rule, these groups were largely allowed to maintain their ethnic identity and religion as long as they followed the party line in politics and economics. This ethnic continuity has preserved traditions and religious beliefs that have in the past existed side by side.

ETHNIC MULTIPLICITY

Like other Balkan countries, North Macedonia's challenge is to incorporate its minority groups into a peaceful and productive society. The constitution, written in 1991, addresses the country's ethnic multiplicity: "Macedonia is constituted as a national country of the Macedonian people which guarantees complete civil equality and permanent mutual living of the Macedonian people with the Albanians, Turks, Vlachs, Roma and the other nationalities living in the Republic of Macedonia." However, North Macedonia suffers from identity problems stemming from conflicts among ethnic groups with differing opportunities and national priorities.

When Pope Francis visited Skopje on May 7, 2019, he urged North Macedonians and all people of the Balkans to embrace ethnic diversity. Even though he does not represent the Eastern Orthodox majority religion in North Macedonia, he was warmly welcomed by the people there.

Ethnic conflicts in this region are not limited to North Macedonia but include the treatment of minorities in other countries as well. Greece maintains that

Pope Francis greets the crowds in Skopje during his visit in 2019.

MACEDONIA° IS AN ANCIENT GREEK WORD
MACEDONIANS WERE GREEKS
MACEDONIA IS GREECE

This is **NO MACEDONIA**
These are **NOT Macedonians**

It's citizens have **NO RELATION** with
Macedonians..**THEY ARE NOT GREEKS**..
Slavs,Albanians,Roms,Turks,are the 98% of its
population.The oldest ,arrived to this area almost 1000
years AFTER Macedonians and Alexander the Great !!

**DISTORTING
HISTORICAL TRUTH**
you and my **TRAITOROUS
GOVERNMENT**
RECOGNISED THIS STATE AS
REPUBLIC OF NORTH MACEDONIA

THIS STATE ARROGATES ALEXANDER the Great
the MACEDON and ANCIENT MACEDONIA.
It uses the term **MACEDONIAN** to characterize its
products,its Slavic language,its **Nationality** and its
multicultural citizens.

The southern part of it WAS ONCE
CAPTURED by ancient Macedonian Kings.
SO was EGYPT and PERSIA ..2500 years ago!!!!
Those areas ,indeed, were parts of a
Macedonian empire. BUT they were NOT
MACEDONIA..

Ancient Macedonia

Empire of Alexander the Great,the Macedon

A banner at a 2019 rally in Thessaloniki, Greece, vehemently spells out arguments against North Macedonia's claim to the name "Macedonia."

its history predates that of the people in North Macedonia who call themselves Macedonians. North Macedonians maintain that this is either not true at all, only partially true, or irrelevant. Greeks maintain that North Macedonians are a threat to stability because of their communist past. Macedonians maintain that the Greeks were too complicit with the Nazis. Greeks maintain that Greek Macedonians are treated badly in North Macedonia. North Macedonia maintains that Albanians and Macedonians are treated badly in Greece.

ALBANIANS IN NORTH MACEDONIA

Another element in North Macedonian identity involves the presence of Albanians, a situation stemming from the creation of Yugoslavia and Albania in the early 20th century, which set borders leaving over half of the people who called themselves Albanian outside of their newly created country. Thousands of them were living in the part of Yugoslavia that is today North Macedonia, and like Bosnian Albanians and Kosovar Albanians, they make their presence and their demands known forcefully.

Today, Albanians comprise between 25 and 33 percent of the North Macedonian population. (No one is certain because there hasn't been a census since 2002 due to political disputes.) Their rights to civil protection and power were enumerated in the NATO-brokered peace agreement of 2001 in hopes that ethnic strife in the country could be eased. The agreement stipulated that what was then Macedonia would amend its constitution to include all ethnic groups, not just Slavic Macedonians, which it did. In addition, Albanian, or Shqip, would be recognized as a second official language in areas where Albanians constitute 20 percent or more of the population. That, too, was accomplished. More vaguely, Albanians were to constitute a larger percentage than before of the police forces and to have a degree of self-rule in areas where they are the majority.

Young ethnic Albanians chant nationalist slogans at a rally in Skopje in 2004.

MOTHER TERESA

Mother Teresa (1910–1997) was an ethnic Albanian Roman Catholic nun who spent most of her life working with the very poor and dying in India. Since 2016, she has been known as Saint Teresa of Calcutta to Roman Catholics worldwide. It is a tribute to Mother Teresa—and to the complexity of Albanian and North Macedonian identity—that North Macedonia, where she was born, and Albania, the home of her people, both claim her as their own.

She was born Agnes Gonxha Bojaxhiu in Skopje in 1910. At that time, Skopje was in the Kosovo Vilayet, a region of the Ottoman Empire. At the age of 18, she joined a convent in Ireland that did missionary work in India. At 21, she took her vows as a nun. For many years, she taught at a high school in Calcutta (now called Kolkata), but she was moved to do more by the suffering of the poor in the streets. Her first mission was an outdoor school for the children of Calcutta's slums, relying only on volunteers for support. In 1948, Mother Teresa founded her own order, the Missionaries of Charity, with the intention of caring for the most desolate and forsaken of people. As word of her mission and her devotion spread throughout the world, she received financial support that enabled her order to open missions in many other countries. In 2015 (after her death), the organization was active in 139 countries.

Mother Teresa received numerous accolades and became internationally famous. In 1979, she was honored with the Nobel Peace Prize. After her death, the Vatican began the process that leads to canonization (sainthood), which requires the documentation of miracles believed to be the result of her intercession after death. In Teresa's case, Catholic authorities accepted the claim of a woman in India who believed she was cured of a stomach tumor on the anniversary of Mother Teresa's death. After recognizing a second miracle attributed to Teresa, Pope Francis canonized the nun in 2016, at which point she became Saint Teresa of Calcutta.

In preparation for these changes, a new census was to be held before the next election to determine ethnic populations and thus award representative power. However, that census, in 2011, was cancelled mid-operation because different interpretations of the surveying methodology could not guarantee reliable data. In short, the Albanians wanted the census to be conducted one way (which would maximize their numbers), and the Macedonians wanted it another way. Political mayhem ensued, and the process was shut down.

For the Albanian Macedonians, their numbers have therefore been in dispute. They have continued to campaign for increased representation and recognition of their needs as a minority in language and religion. Some of their demands have been met, but mistrust and dissatisfaction are ongoing.

The majority of Albanians are Muslims. However, there are some exceptions—some Orthodox Christian Albanians live in a few villages around Lake Ohrid and the town of Struga, and some Roman Catholics live in the area around Skopje. The late Mother Teresa is the best known among the Roman Catholics from Macedonia.

TURKS

The Turks are the second-largest minority in Macedonia. Like other ethnic groups, they claim higher numbers than the census shows, somewhere between 170,000 and 200,000. The government estimates them at around 100,000. Once there were many more, but when the Ottoman Empire fell at the beginning of the 20th century, many fled to Turkey. Under Yugoslav rule, more left after World War II. Others intermarried or simply identified themselves as Macedonians or Albanians to avoid stigma and persecution. Most Turks are Muslims.

ROMA

The Roma (or Romani) people probably originated in India and migrated to the Balkans during the Ottoman conquest. Most of them are Muslims. The Roma are an ethnic minority and, like most minorities in Macedonia, claim to have been undercounted in the 2002 census, which put their number at

54,000. Many of the Roma live in a neighborhood in Skopje called Suto Orizari (or Shutka to locals), where they make up 80 percent of the population. It is possibly the only district in Europe where Roma are a majority. More than 6,000 Roma refugees came to Macedonia as victims of warfare in Kosovo. Like the Serbs and some other refugees from Kosovo, many were reluctant to return home, even after the conflict diminshed.

Roma in North Macedonia, as elsewhere in the world, are a besieged minority. Formerly called gypsies—the term is now considered derogatory—they rarely intermarry or mix with people of other backgrounds. Traditionally, they were gifted musicians and craftsmen, working in leather, metals, and fibers. They served as repairmen and performed at weddings and other celebrations. However, the Roma generally live in poverty in cities, where they are often homeless or, at best, transients. Women and children often beg for money from tourists, though not from North Macedonians, who are immune to their pleas.

International aid efforts are aimed at encouraging the Roma to send their children to school—only 11 percent of North Macedonian Roma have received some form of higher education, compared to 60 percent of all citizens—and at discouraging discrimination by outsiders.

Two Macedonian Roma pull an old car shell with their horse cart in Skopje.

VLACHS

Since the second century, the Vlachs have been in North Macedonia, making them the country's oldest ethnic group. Most of their settlements were along the Via Egnatia, the Roman trade route, where they were tradesmen and shepherds. They speak, as they always have, a Latin-based language, and they call themselves Aromani, after their place of origin in today's Romania. Today, they are mostly urban people, often operating successful businesses and hotels.

Many do not identify themselves as anything other than North Macedonian, and those that do constitute only 0.5 percent of the population.

OTHER MINORITIES

The Torbeshi are a Slavic, Macedonian-speaking population that converted to Islam during the Ottoman period. There are also Bosnians in North Macedonia, some of whom trace their roots in the country back to the 19th century. Throughout the period of ethnic persecution in Serbia, Bosnia, and Kosovo, refugees fled to Macedonia. By 2004, most of them had returned home to relative safety, but the enormous flow in and out of the country, combined with the lack of a recent census, has left numbers unusually hard to determine.

CONFLICTS WITH NEIGHBORING COUNTRIES

It's not surprising, perhaps, that in a part of the world where invasions, conversions, and conquests were frequent and bloody, North Macedonians and their neighbors have sometimes had harsh words for each other. Demosthenes, the Greek orator and historian, denounced Philip II, the father of Alexander the Great, as "not only not a Greek nor related to the Greeks, but not even a barbarian from a land worth mentioning; no, he's a pestilence from Macedonia, a region where you can't even buy a slave worth his salt." Despite this evaluation of his father, Alexander the Great has always been considered a Greek hero.

Into the 21st century, Greece opposed Macedonia's name and of the Star of Vergina, or the Vergina Sun, the 16-rayed star symbol that decorates the golden larnax, a box found in a burial site in Vergina, Greece, in 1977 that is believed to have belonged to King Philip II of Macedon, the very man reviled

A banner on a statue of Alexander the Great in Greece protests against the name "North Macedonia."

The eight-rayed North Macedonian flag waves against a sunny blue sky.

by Demosthenes. Archaeologists do not agree whether the sun was a symbol of the Macedonian state, a symbol of Philip's dynasty, a religious symbol, or simply a decorative design. Eight-pointed suns often appear on Macedonian coins and shields of that period. Eight-, twelve- and (rarely) sixteen-pointed suns have been used as a decorative element in Greece for centuries. Macedonia conceded the use of the Vergina Sun on its flag when it joined the United Nations. An eight-pointed sun is the current design on the flag. Greece displays the Vergina Sun as the official symbol of the Greek province of Macedonia.

Language has also been used as a club to coerce people into a new ethnic identity. Under Serbian rule during the 1920s and 1930s, the Slavs in Vardar Macedonia were regarded as southern Serbs and the language they spoke was regarded as a southern Serbian dialect. In addition to closing Bulgarian, Greek, and Romanian schools, the Serbs expelled Bulgarian priests and all non-Serbian teachers, reducing the influence of other languages. Bulgarian surnames ending in —ov and —ev were replaced with names with the Serbian ending —ich. Throughout the 20th century, people living in Bulgaria and Greece exposed themselves to discrimination and danger by identifying themselves as Macedonian, as their ethnicity was officially declared nonexistent.

Albania recognizes a population of 10,000 ethnic Macedonians living within its borders (Macedonians claim at least 10 times as many). However, in the region of Golo Bardo, near the North Macedonian border, there are two Slavic organizations, one Bulgarian and the other Macedonian. Each claims the Slavic population there for itself, with the Bulgarian organization saying they are Bulgarian and the Macedonian organization saying they are Macedonian. The population itself, which is predominantly Muslim, has chosen to call itself Albanian in the official census, avoiding the dispute and removing themselves from the Slavic count altogether.

The ultimate conflict over language and ethnicity finds its expression in the country's name. When Macedonia was admitted to the United Nations in 1993, its name was officially entered as "the Former Yugoslav Republic of Macedonia (FYROM)" in a concession to Greece, which maintained that its northern province was the only place entitled to use the name Macedonia.

That decision did not sit well with the Slavic population of the new nation, who compared it to calling the United States "the Former Colonies of Great Britain in North America." For years, Greece was able to enforce the use of the more cumbersome FYROM name among European Union nations, which require a consensus for any decision. Therefore, even though the other EU countries approved of inviting Macedonia to join the organization, Greece successfully blocked Macedonia's use of the name until the 2018 Prespa Agreement.

INTERNET LINKS

https://www.biography.com/religious-figure/mother-teresa
This site offers a well-balanced portrait of Mother Teresa's life and accomplishments.

https://www.euronews.com/2018/07/05/only-district-in-europe -roma-are-majority
This article highlights the Roma neighborhood of Skopje.

LIFESTYLE

A hiker climbs a high hillside of Mount Korab.

7

FAMILY AND FRIENDSHIP FORM THE fabric of the North Macedonian way of life. People take seriously the need to do each other small favors and to extend and receive hospitality. These expressions of respect and affection are repeated throughout a lifetime to weave ties that bind through generations. Conversations are lively and often emotional, as people passionately express opinions based on long-held beliefs.

North Macedonians welcome visitors to their homes and will typically invite them to stay for a meal. To refuse such an invitation is to offer insult. Older guests are especially honored and are served food first and expected to lead conversations while others listen.

Society has gone from 90 percent rural in the mid-20th century to about 60 percent urban. Families, traditionally large, have become smaller in recent years; in 2018, the country had a fertility rate of 1.49 children per woman, a relatively low rate (198th out of 224 countries). Albanian families are an exception, and they tend to be nearly twice the size of the national average.

The Orthodox Christian Church is very influential in the lives of its members, providing religious services and rituals for all of life's events. In Christian towns, the church calendar provides the basis of family and

North Macedonia has adopted several laws to advance gender equality. The Law on Equal Opportunities of Women and Men, adopted in 2006, requires public institutions to ensure equal rights and opportunities for women and men and to actively work to reduce gender inequality. Nevertheless, gender inequalities continue, and more work needs to be done.

Pedestrians stroll while others relax at outdoor café tables on the streets of the Old Bazaar area of Skopje.

community life, with Orthodox holidays and feast days, and also with saints' days unique to each town. Even historical celebrations usually center on the church. In Muslim communities, likewise, much of the activity centers on the mosque, but the baths and the market are also central.

Over half the people in North Macedonia live in cities, nearly a quarter of them in or around the capital city of Skopje. Though population numbers regarding ethnic composition are sometimes questioned, officially about two-thirds of the North Macedonians are of Macedonian descent, a quarter to one-third are Albanian, and the remainder are Turks, Roma, Serbs, Vlachs, and other ethnic groups. The average life expectancy at birth has risen to 78.2 years for women and 73.8 years for men. The poverty rate has risen precipitously, from less than 4 percent in 1991 to 21.5 percent in 2015, with unemployment and the impact of global refugees largest among the causes.

EDUCATION

Education is available to everyone and is compulsory from the ages of 6 to 15, through the equivalent of eighth grade. Four years of high school are available, but not required. Often the high schools focus training on the economic and vocational needs of the area.

Education in North Macedonia is as multilingual as its population. Primary education is in one of four languages, depending on location—Macedonian, Albanian, Turkish, or Serbo-Croatian. Within the schools, most children are separated ethnically, and it is unusual for them to socialize outside their groups. Still, there are those who would break down the ethnic barriers. For example, a program called Appreciating Differences was designed to bring groups of students from ethnically mixed high schools together to discuss multiculturalism, human rights, stereotypes, prejudice, and discrimination.

There are 21 higher education institutions in the country, out of which 7 are public universities. In recent years, the number of students attending

Schoolchildren work at their desks in an elementary classroom in Skopje.

North Macedonian universities has been steadily increasing. In the 2014/2015 academic year, there were roughly 60,000 students, most of them at the public institutions. The public Saints Cyril and Methodius University in Skopje is the largest facility of higher education in the country. The University of Saint Clement of Ohrid at Bitola is another important state university. South East European University in Tetovo offers classes in Albanian, Macedonian, and English.

THE STREETS OF NORTH MACEDONIA

The old and the new exist side by side in North Macedonia. Medieval churches and mosques, some converted from one to the other and then back again, dot the country's towns and city streets. In Skopje, modern malls in the new part of town contrast with the old Turkish market across the river. People can buy American-style fast food from chains, or they can get homemade cheese pies, or *bureks* (BOO-recks), and yogurt from local street sellers. Young women in

Open umbrellas hang between buildings to provide shade while also adding to the festive atmosphere in the Old Bazaar section of Skopje.

In April 2019, authorities in North Macedonia declared a national measles epidemic after noting more than 900 cases of the disease just since the start of the year. Three infants in the country had died of complications from the disease. Measles is a preventable disease, and a vaccine exists. However, it can be deadly for infants who are too young to receive the vaccine and for people with compromised health.

According to the World Health Organization (WHO), incidents of the highly contagious disease have risen dramatically worldwide. In 2017, the most recent year for which estimates are available, WHO said measles caused "close to 110,000 deaths" worldwide. Health experts in North Macedonia blamed the growing anti-vaccination ("anti-vax") movement. Vaccination rates have been falling in North Macedonia since 2014. Through social media, the anti-vax movement spread through North Macedonia, causing parents to fear and distrust the vaccination process. The country's Public Health Institute reported that more than 11,000 North Macedonian preschool children had not been vaccinated.

In an effort to step up vaccinations, the government barred unvaccinated children from attending school, thereby enforcing an existing Health Protection Law. That did not sit well with North Macedonia's anti-vax parents, who demanded the barrier to school be rescinded.

Men sit and chat at outdoor tables under trees and umbrellas.

Western-style jeans and T-shirts pass observant Muslim women who cover their faces with black veils in public.

Traditionally, bargaining has played a role in North Macedonian enterprises. Traders tend to start high and work their way down to acceptable levels of expected return. North Macedonians see bargaining as a process and a skill, and they are very good at it. Outsiders must expect to be tested when they do business.

Tradition and unemployment keep the many cafés and coffee houses full from morning to night with men looking for company and a way to pass the time. Strong Turkish coffee, sometimes called Macedonian coffee, is the drink of choice, served in tiny cups or glasses.

Some city neighborhoods have a modern, hipster vibe about them, with trendy cafés and boutique shops. Others seem right out of an earlier time period. This quirky mix makes for charming and interesting street life.

North Macedonia has more sheep than people, and the business of shepherding is as old as the mountains. Shepherds in the region have a unique dog, once known only to them and to the wolves. Legend says that eagles and falcons spread tales about these heroic dogs and their battles with the wild mountain beasts.

Formerly known as the Ilyrian shepherd dog, or Yugoslav shepherd, the Sarplaninac (shar-plan-EEN-atz) is an ancient dog breed still widely used in the mountains to protect flocks against predators. Its name derives from the Sar Mountains. According to legend, it was once unknown outside the mountains, and in fact, it could not even be exported from Yugoslavia until 1950.

Now, it is a recognized breed and is sold in both the United States and Canada. Sarplaninacs are medium-sized dogs by breeding standards, about 2 feet (0.6 m) tall at the shoulder and weighing between 65 and 100 pounds (30 and 45 kg) at maturity, but they seem much bigger because of their heavy bones and thick coats. Most often, they are tones of gray, but they can be fawn as well, and in the mountains, they are often mixed colors. Though they are smaller than many other sheepdog breeds, Sarplaninacs are terrifically strong and have very large teeth. Their loyalty, intelligence, and initiative make them superb guard dogs. They are calm dogs generally, but they are fearless and react quickly and courageously when they sense a threat. Their speed and demeanor can turn back a bear or a wolf.

Rainbow-colored streamers decorate an umbrella in the first LGBT+ pride parade in Skopje in 2019.

SOCIAL ISSUES

Unfavorable political, economic, and social conditions have increasingly resulted in a decline in the standard of living, reduced government services, high unemployment, and rising health problems, especially among ethnic minorities. The rates of drug addiction and other social problems have risen. Without adequate funding, the social services required to help people in trouble are sorely lacking.

One result is that increasing numbers of young people are looking abroad for their future. With professors, doctors, and other professionals in North

Macedonia being extremely low-paid, educated young adults know they can earn better money in other countries.

Regarding LGBT+ rights, same-sex marriage was not recognized in North Macedonia as of 2019. Same-sex households were not eligible for any of the same legal protections as those of heterosexual married couples. However, discrimination on the grounds of sexual orientation or gender identity was prohibited by new legislation in 2019. Nevertheless, society in general has not caught up to the law in that matter. According to a World Bank study, North Macedonia is one of the least accepting countries in the region toward LGBT+ people. In June 2019, around 1,000 people participated in the first-ever LGBT+ pride demonstration in Skopje, and some state officials and foreign diplomats joined the march.

INTERNET LINKS

**https://www.aljazeera.com/ajimpact/north-macedonia-battles
-youth-brain-drain-190813151030745.html**
This article highlights the problem of professionals and young people seeking employment outside of their country.

**https://borgenproject.org/top-10-facts-about-living-conditions
-in-macedonia**
This site gives an overview of everyday life in North Macedonia.

https://www.petguide.com/breeds/dog/sarplaninac
The Sarplaninac dog is discussed on this pet site.

https://rainbow-europe.org/#8646/0/0
Rainbow Europe, a leading LGBT+ rights organization, ranks North Macedonia's progress on human rights relating to sexual orientation and gender.

RELIGION

The Church of Saint John at Kaneo, overlooking Lake Ohrid, is an iconic Orthodox Christian site in North Macedonia.

NORTH MACEDONIA IS A LARGELY Christian nation, with its own independent church in the Eastern Orthodox tradition. However, it has a sizable Muslim minority, which presents a challenge in unifying the country.

In the ninth century CE, the creation of the first Slavic alphabet resulted in the spread of Christianity among the Slavic people. For the first time, a Slavonic ecclesiastical organization could use the Slavic language instead of Greek in religious services. The flowering of Macedonian culture that grew out of the Ohrid Literary School, the first Slavonic university, led to the Macedonian Orthodox Church.

The Macedonian Orthodox Church ministers to two-thirds of North Macedonia's citizens. Most of the others practice the Muslim faith. A tiny minority is Roman Catholic or another religion.

MACEDONIAN ORTHODOX CHURCH

Through the centuries, the Orthodox Church has stimulated and supported the national identity of the Macedonian people. Always on the forefront of resistance and uprisings against the Bulgarian and Ottoman Empires, it also provided education, especially linguistic and literary.

In 893 CE, the Macedonian Orthodox Church was established in Ohrid, with Saint Clement, one of its founders, as its first archbishop. Saint Clement and Saint Naum, disciples of Saint Cyril and Saint Methodius, carried on the teachings of their mentors, taking as their mission the

8

The largest cathedral in North Macedonia is the Church of Saint Clement of Ohrid in Skopje, which was completed in 1990. The oldest church in the country is the Church of Saint Sophia in Ohrid, which dates to the 6th century CE but was rebuilt in the 10th century. During the rule of the Ottoman Empire, it functioned as a mosque. Perhaps the most photographed church is that of Saint John at Kaneo, which dates to the 13th century and overlooks Lake Ohrid.

The recently renovated Church of Saints Clement and Panteleimon in Ohrid is thought to have been designed by Saint Clement himself.

education of their people in the Macedonian language and the establishments of schools throughout the country.

Though the church was taken over by the Greek clergy upon the fall of the Macedonians to the Byzantine Empire in 1018, it continued to unite the Macedonians until it was officially abolished by the Turks in 1786. In 1945, the Republic of Yugoslavia allowed it to be revived, though politics made membership undesirable. Once again, the church assumed a central role in supporting a national identity.

Today's Macedonian Orthodox Church harkens back to the days of Saint Clement's archbishopric of Ohrid. Once again it is centered in Ohrid, where it is headed by the archbishop of Ohrid and North Macedonia and the Holy Synod of Bishops, which consists of six bishops. North Macedonia has more than

The Eastern Orthodox Church, or Orthodox Catholic Church, is a Christian branch that separated from the Roman Catholic Church in the year 1054. The split between the two churches was related to the division of the Roman Empire into Eastern and Western halves, the Eastern center being the city of Constantinople (now known as Istanbul) and the Western center being Rome. Conflict over issues of doctrine led to an irreconcilable division, and the patriarch of Constantinople and the pope of Rome excommunicated each other. Following this divorce, the two branches went in quite distinct directions, largely due to the different cultures of the West and the East.

Bartholomew I has been the ecumenical patriarch of Constantinople since 1991.

Eastern Orthodox Christianity is widely practiced in Greece, Eastern and Southeastern Europe, and Russia. The Orthodox Church is a communion of 14 officially recognized autocephalous (that is, independent, self-administered) regional churches, with the ecumenical patriarch of Constantinople as the honorary figurehead. The Macedonian Orthodox Church is not one of these officially recognized churches but rather is viewed by Orthodox authorities as an offshoot of the Serbian Orthodox Church.

One difference between Roman Catholicism and Eastern Orthodoxy is that the latter does not recognize an authority figure on par with the Catholic pope. The patriarch of Constantinople—the highest ranking bishop—does not have the powers of a pope. Another is that mysticism is extremely important to Eastern Orthodox Christianity. The faithful view prayer and spirituality as mystical experiences that can range from ecstatic union with the "divine energies" of God to deep contemplation of scripture.

The Eastern Orthodox Church (like the Roman Catholic Church) considers itself to be the "one, holy, catholic, and apostolic church" established by Christ and his apostles.

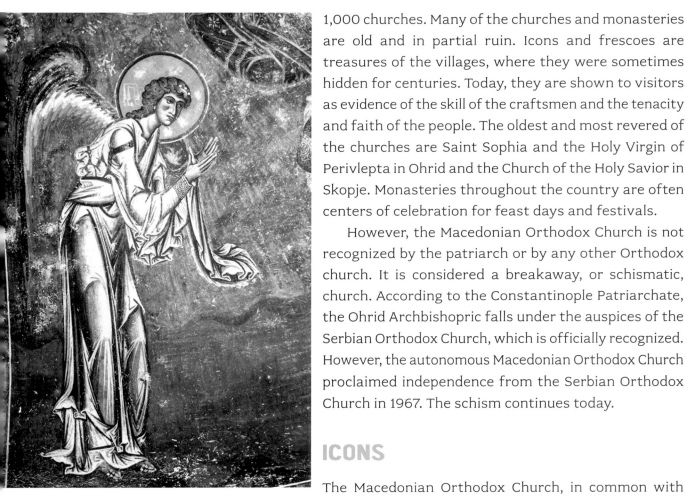

A fresco of the Archangel Gabriel adorns a wall in the Church of Saint George in the village of Kurbinovo.

1,000 churches. Many of the churches and monasteries are old and in partial ruin. Icons and frescoes are treasures of the villages, where they were sometimes hidden for centuries. Today, they are shown to visitors as evidence of the skill of the craftsmen and the tenacity and faith of the people. The oldest and most revered of the churches are Saint Sophia and the Holy Virgin of Perivlepta in Ohrid and the Church of the Holy Savior in Skopje. Monasteries throughout the country are often centers of celebration for feast days and festivals.

However, the Macedonian Orthodox Church is not recognized by the patriarch or by any other Orthodox church. It is considered a breakaway, or schismatic, church. According to the Constantinople Patriarchate, the Ohrid Archbishopric falls under the auspices of the Serbian Orthodox Church, which is officially recognized. However, the autonomous Macedonian Orthodox Church proclaimed independence from the Serbian Orthodox Church in 1967. The schism continues today.

ICONS

The Macedonian Orthodox Church, in common with all Eastern Orthodox churches, places great importance on icons, or holy images. Usually, these are flat panel paintings illuminated by candles. An icon is traditionally regarded as a kind of window between the earthly and the spiritual worlds, a window through which an inhabitant of the celestial world—a saint, or Jesus Christ himself—looks into the human world. The image recorded in the icon is a sacred one because of the belief that the true features of the heavenly spirit have somehow been imprinted in a two-dimensional way on the icon. This belief in the sacred nature of an icon was developed by early religious scholars in the eighth and ninth centuries into the concept of incarnation. The idea was that Jesus Christ becomes incarnate in the very

materials of the icon—the wood, plaster, paint, and oils. The veneration shown to an icon is not worship of the object itself but rather of the divine image as glorified by the object. That understanding helps to explain the extraordinary reverence accorded to icons in the religion.

A believer goes up to the iconostasis—the wall of paintings that separates the front and rear of the church—and kisses the icons. On the feast day of a particular saint, the icon of that saint is displayed on the lectern, where the faithful pay their respects with a kiss and a bow. Then, they make the sign of the cross before rejoining the congregation.

At home, an Orthodox family usually has an icon hanging in the eastern corner of the living room and another in the bedroom. Traditionally, a guest on entering a room first greets the icon by making the sign of the cross and bowing to it.

Golden icons grace the iconostasis of the Macedonian Orthodox church at the Monastery of Saint Naum in Ohrid.

The Eastern Orthodox Church (also referred to as the Byzantine Church), like Protestantism, rejects the belief that the pope is infallible. Roman Catholics believe that when it comes to theological matters, the pope cannot make a mistake. There are also other areas where the two branches of the Catholic Church disagree. However, on other essential matters, the Orthodox Church shares many basic tenets of faith with the Roman Catholic Church, including these:

TRINITY   The Holy Trinity is the idea that God is one indivisible God made up of three distinct divine "persons"—the Father, the Son, and the Holy Spirit. The nature of the Trinity is understood to be a mystery, beyond human comprehension, and accessible only through spiritual experience.

RESURRECTION OF CHRIST The life, death, and resurrection (coming back to life after death) of Jesus Christ are understood to be real, historic events as described in the Gospels of the New Testament. Jesus is seen as the Son of God, both human and divine.

TRANSUBSTANTIATION   This is the belief that in the celebration of the Eucharist, or Holy Communion, ordinary bread and wine are literally—not just symbolically—transformed into the body and blood of Jesus Christ.

AFTERLIFE   After a person dies, it is believed that the soul is separated from the body and resides in either Paradise (Heaven) or Hades (Hell). Unlike Roman Catholicism, the Orthodox Church does not accept the concept of Purgatory, a transitional state between the two. Both Churches believe that the soul and body will be reunited at the time of the Final Judgment.

Icons often appear mysterious to both the faithful and nonbelievers. As a form of art, icons have no concept of authorship. This is one of the differences between the art of the icon and the art of Western Christianity. For centuries, the Eastern Orthodox Church has been content to repeat certain types of sacred images. The craft of producing icons was done in monasteries, with a group of monks working together on one icon. One monk might work on the eyes or hair, while another would devote himself to painting the robes of the figure being represented. Icon painters (iconographers) prepared themselves for painting through fasting, prayer, and Holy Communion because it was believed that to paint Jesus Christ better, one must have a close relationship with God. Today, some iconographers are specially trained laypeople.

During the eighth and ninth centuries, partly through the influence of Islam, an opposition to images in worship began to pervade the Eastern Orthodox Church. During the annual Feast of Orthodoxy, instituted in 842 CE, the entire Orthodox Church celebrates and honors the victory of those who supported the use of icons during worship over the iconoclasts—those who opposed the use of icons.

The richly embellished walls shown here are only a part of the awe-inspiring decorated interior of Tetovo's famous Painted Mosque.

ISLAM IN NORTH MACEDONIA

About one-quarter to one-third of Macedonia's citizens are Muslim, and the great majority of these are ethnic Albanians. Most live in the west and the northwest, near the Kosovar and Albanian borders, and in the city of Skopje. Mosques throughout the land provide architectural history of the rule of the Ottoman Empire. Most of the mosques to be seen today were built in the 15th and 16th centuries. The Isa Bey Mosque, the Mustafa Pasha Mosque, and the Sultan Murat Mosque in Skopje, and the Sarena Mosque, or Painted Mosque, in Tetovo are the among the most famous and beautiful.

The ornate exterior of the Painted Mosque hints at the elaborate decoration within.

While the Macedonian Orthodox Church benefited from the tolerance of the Yugoslav government, the Muslims of Macedonia received treatment that was less favorable, as they were perceived to be less amenable to Yugoslav unity. Since the creation of the Macedonian Republic in 1991, mistrust has persisted between officials of the two religions. Once a part of the Islamic community administered from Sarajevo in Bosnia and Herzegovina, the Macedonian Islamic community is today centered in Skopje.

The Muslims in the Republic of North Macedonia are ethnically and religiously heterogeneous. Ethnically, they are the Albanians, Turks, Macedonian Muslims (Torbeshi), Bosnians, and Roma, with the Albanians in the majority.

BASIC TENETS OF ISLAM

Islam means "submission to God" (Allah), and those who submit to Allah are known as Muslims. The fundamental belief of Muslims is that "there is no god but God (Allah) and Muhammad is his Prophet." Muslims repeat this testimony sincerely during many rituals. The revelations made by Allah to Muhammad are recorded in the Quran, the Muslim sacred book, and are considered to bring to completion the series of biblical revelations received by Jews and Christians.

Islam stands on five pillars: to witness that there is no God but Allah and that Muhammad is his Prophet; to perform the required prayers; to pay the *zakat* (ZAHR-cut), or charity dues; to fast during the month of Ramadan; and to perform the pilgrimage to Mecca (the *hajj*).

Whenever possible, men pray together at a mosque under an imam, and on Fridays they are obliged to do so. Women also worship at the mosque, where they are segregated from the men. They may also pray in seclusion at home.

INTERNET LINKS

https://balkaninsight.com/2014/10/01/cross-and-crescent-divide-up-macedonia
This article looks at how the construction of new churches and mosques reveals religious tensions in North Macedonia.

http://www.mpc.org.mk/English/default.asp
This is the English-language home site of the Macedonian Orthodox Church.

https://www.nytimes.com/2019/05/07/world/europe/pope-francis-north-macedonia.html
This article looks at Pope Francis's visit to North Macedonia in 2019.

https://www.rferl.org/a/29551213.html
The article "Will Macedonia's Orthodox Church Also Break Away?" focuses on the schism in the Eastern Orthodox Church.

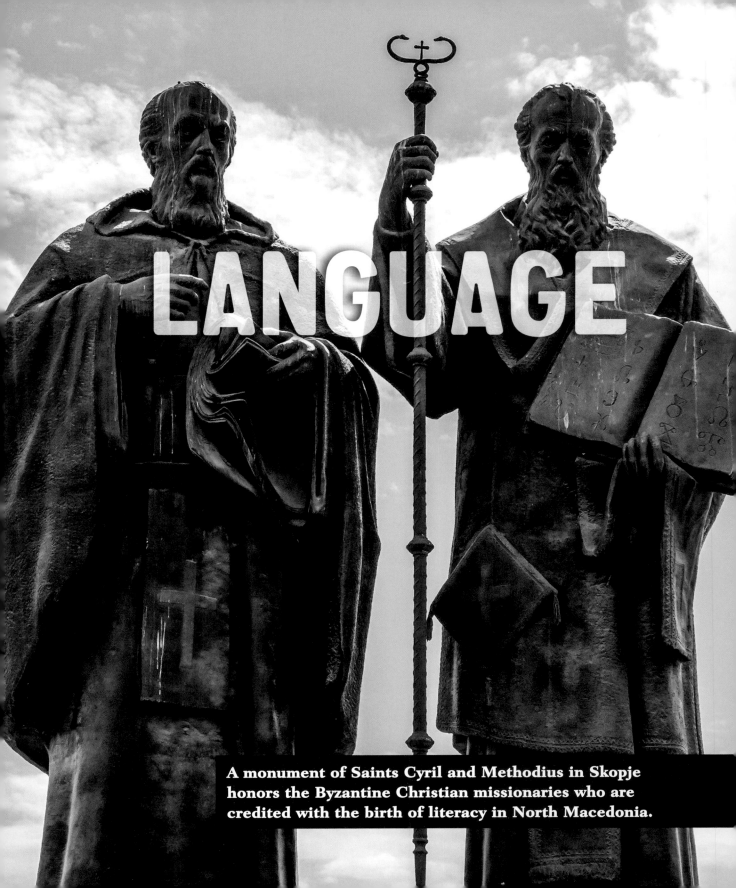

LANGUAGE

A monument of Saints Cyril and Methodius in Skopje honors the Byzantine Christian missionaries who are credited with the birth of literacy in North Macedonia.

9

LANGUAGE IS A FUNDAMENTAL PART of the North Macedonian identity. Throughout centuries of occupation, invaders have recognized this fact and have worked hard to suppress, outlaw, corrupt, or otherwise weaken the language and thus its role. In the past century, Serbs attempted to weaken the use of Macedonian by introducing Serbian into the schools and government. Macedonians in northern Greece were also forbidden to speak Macedonian by a repressive government in the 1930s.

Though it belongs to the Slavic family of languages and shares some characteristics of the languages of neighboring countries like Bulgaria, Albania, and Serbia, Macedonian is nevertheless a unique language. It has been a written language since the ninth century, but its first written grammar did not appear until 1946. Even without a codified grammar, however, church documents, linguistic studies, scientific treatises, literature, and translations from other languages were created in the Macedonian language.

The Macedonian language and alphabet are governed by rules and regularities, standardized in 1903. Its 31 letters are pronounced in only one way, no matter how they are combined. Another regularity governs

Macedonian is a Slavic language. Others in this category include Belarusian, Bulgarian, Czech, Polish, Russian, Serbo-Croatian, Slovak, Slovenian, and Ukrainian.

An information board regarding the excavations in the ancient Roman village of Stobi in Gradsko, North Macedonia, is written in both Latin and Cyrillic scripts.

accenting syllables—the third to last syllable always gets the accent. In shorter words, the first or only syllable is accented. These two rules make the language easy to speak. Here are some simple words and phrases in Macedonian:

hello . . . . *zdavo* (ZDAH-voh)
yes . . . . *da* (DAH)
no . . . . *ne* (NEH)
please . . . . *molam* (MOH-lahm)
thank you . . . . . . *blagodaram* (blah-GO-dah-ram)
How are you? . . . . . *Kako si?* (KAH-ko SEE?)

CYRILLIC SCRIPT

Like many other languages in Eastern Europe and northern Eurasia, Macedonian—or македонски—is written in the Cyrillic script. As with the Latin alphabet, it is written and read left to right. The letters are based on the earliest Slavic script known as Glagolitic, an early writing system created in the ninth century by the brothers Cyril and Methodius. They were Byzantine Christian missionaries who worked to convert the Slavic people to Christianity. In order to translate the Bible into the local language, they devised an early version of the Cyrillic (after Cyril) alphabet. Through their work, they also laid the groundwork for Macedonian literacy, and a monument to them stands today in Skopje. Their disciples Clement and Naum of Ohrid went on to establish the first Slavonic university, the Ohrid Literary School, which eventually graduated over 3,500 teachers, clergymen, philosophers, and other writers.

The Cyrillic alphabet is closely based on the Greek alphabet, with about a dozen additional letters invented to represent Slavic sounds not found in Greek. Early manuscripts show no difference between uppercase and lowercase letters, but today's Cyrillic does. However, the lowercase letters are mostly—though not all—just smaller versions of the uppercase style. The script also has a cursive style. Cyrillic is similar, but not identical, in all the languages that use it, and there are numerous alphabets using the script.

ROMANIZATION

The need to translate Cyrillic Macedonian into a form understandable by people who use the Latin, or Roman, alphabet led to a method for its transliteration. (The Latin alphabet is the one used in English and the languages of Western Europe.) The Romanized version of Macedonian is simply Macedonian written in the Latin alphabet, according to an official transliteration system of substituting letter forms. The Romanized form is required on all passports.

ALBANIAN

With roughly one-quarter to one-third of its people being Albanian, Macedonia has recognized the Albanian language as an official language of the country. In areas where more than 20 percent of the people speak Albanian, or Shqip, signage and government documents are in both languages.

Most languages evolve as parts of linguistic families, with similarities in grammar and vocabulary to older or neighboring languages, but not Albanian. Though it has a few words in common with Greek, Latin, and Italian, it is a language without relatives or ancestors.

The Albanian language has 36 letters written in the Latin alphabet, and like Macedonian, it has only been codified in the last century. It has two dialects,

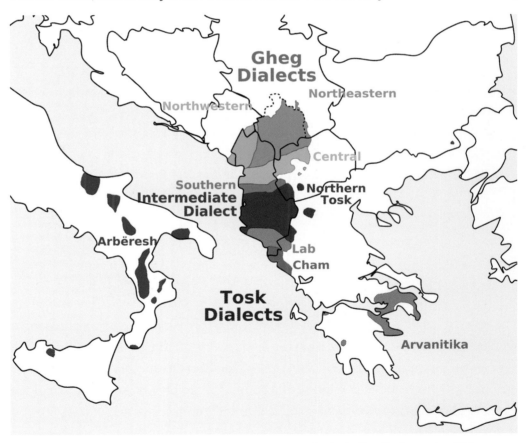

This map shows the range of Albanian-language dialects, including their reach within North Macedonia.

the Gheg of the north and the Tosk of southern Albania. The literary language, however, is mostly taken from the Tosk dialect.

OTHER LANGUAGES

Besides Macedonian and Albanian, many young people in North Macedonia speak English. Older Macedonians are more likely to speak German as a second language. Though different languages, Macedonian and Bulgarian have enough in common that most people can understand both.

INTERNET LINKS

https://www.britannica.com/topic/Albanian-language
The online encyclopedia has an overview of the Albanian language.

https://www.omniglot.com/writing/macedonian.htm
This language site offers an introduction to Macedonian with audio clips and a video.

**https://theculturetrip.com/europe/macedonia/articles/
is-macedonian-one-of-the-oldest-languages-in-the-world**
This travel site provides a good history of the Macedonian language, with photos of Skopje.

ARTS

Beautiful rugs and other textiles are presented
for sale in a handicraft stall in Skopje.

10

THE MULTIPLICITY OF PEOPLES IN North Macedonia has enriched its arts for centuries. Despite the tolls taken by earthquakes, foreign occupations, time, and poverty, icons, architecture, music, poetry, and dance offer testimony to the talent and imagination of the North Macedonian people.

The country has a philharmonic and several other professional orchestras. There are also numerous amateur cultural, artistic, and educational associations throughout the country. Some perform or present programs in Albanian, Turkish, or Romani. Each year, local organizations present performances, concerts, evenings of folk music, exhibitions, and other events. These organizations are central to preserving the traditional dances and music of North Macedonia, passing on knowledge about songs, dances, and musical instruments.

ARCHITECTURE

The longtime presence of Byzantine, Turkish, and Slavic peoples has left layers of civilization, and this is nowhere more apparent than in North Macedonia's architecture. To a great extent, the talents of the builders and craftsmen are expressed in religious buildings—sometimes, as in the case of the Church of Saint Sophia in Ohrid, in layers of influence and history. Many of the buildings are in partial ruin. Poverty and national priorities have not always favored preservation, but dereliction has

"Skopje 2014" was a pet project of Prime Minister Nikola Gruevski. The controversial venture aimed to beautify the city by giving it a nationalistic, neoclassical identity suggesting ties to antiquity. Critics called the project expensive and in poor taste, and in 2018, after Gruevski's resignation, it was halted. Nevertheless, it did produce the city's gigantic statue of Alexander the Great, the Art Bridge, and new government buildings.

exposed former incarnations in some of the buildings—layers of painting, foundations of previous buildings, and additions constructed centuries after the primary edifice.

During the flowering of Macedonian culture in the ninth century, Christians built cathedrals and churches all over the country. The style was Byzantine, with glorious icons and altars and three- or four-nave construction. Many of these beautiful buildings still survive, some having been turned first into mosques and then back into churches. At its Christian height during the 14th to the 16th centuries, Macedonia had more than 1,000 churches and monasteries, designed often in relative isolation from current trends to suit the terrain. In and around Ohrid, for example, churches cling to cliffs and hillsides, perch on high peaks, and even overlook the lake from caves.

MONASTERIES   The monasteries of Macedonia have been central to the lives of its people since the ninth century. Today, there are still many working

The Monastery of Saint Naum overlooks Lake Ohrid.

monasteries, some in Debar, Ohrid, and Prilep. The Monastery of Treskavec in Prilep is featured in the 1994 Academy Award—nominated film *Before the Rain*. In Debar is the Nunnery of Saint Gjorgi Pobedonoset, also known as Saint George the Dragon Slayer, the patron saint of England.

SECULAR STRUCTURES   Byzantine secular buildings of significance were usually fortresses. Remains of the Fortress of Ohrid still stand in the city that Roman historians once referred to as a "city of fortresses." The Fortress of Ohrid is the oldest and best preserved in the country, with 18 towers and 4 gates remaining. Skopje Fortress is also a preserved fortress, built at least in part in the year 535 CE with stones from the ruined town of Skupi, which had been destroyed by an earthquake in 518.

OTTOMAN BUILDINGS   The Ottoman Empire put an end to the construction of churches and fortresses and gave rise to a new type of settlement, based

Samuel's Fortress in the Old Town section of Ohrid dates to the 10th century, during the rule of Czar Samuel of Bulgaria.

on open clusters of houses, inns, baths, and mosques. By the end of the 16th century, for example, there were more than 70 mosques in Bitola. The so-called Painted Mosque, built in Tetovo in the 15th century, is a beautiful example of Ottoman architecture and ornamentation.

ARCHAEOLOGY

North Macedonia's antiquities are world-renowned. Museums in many countries house historical, archaeological, and artistic collections that were bought or seized from Macedonia by invaders and traders throughout the centuries. Even today, nearly every turn in the road brings a view of a building, wall, or road that dates at least in part from centuries past. Remnants of the ancient cities of Stobi (Gradsko), Heraclea Lyncestis (Bitola), Lihnidos (Ohrid), and Skupi (Skopje) are still visible and sometimes central to today's cities. Many such sites now house museums, mosques, and churches. Archaeologists continue

The richly colored interior dome of the Saint Jovan Bigorski (John the Baptist) Monastery in Debar, North Macedonia, is shown here.

to unearth remains of civilization from the Roman and early Christian eras. Churches like Saint Clement's and Panteleimon's in Ohrid date back to the times of Saint Clement in the ninth century. Islamic culture is memorialized in the monuments, bazaars, and baths of the Turkish occupation. The Church of the Holy Savior (also known as the Church of the Ascension of Jesus) in Skopje and the Saint Jovan Bigorski (John the Baptist) Monastery in Debar draw admirers from around the world. Meanwhile, during the period known as the "Macedonian Renaissance" in the 18th and 19th centuries, new monuments and churches were built.

Besides these structural remains, which are the handiwork of master builders and mosaic artisans, there are icons, frescoes, paintings, and carvings on the walls and ceilings of many of the old buildings. Some of the best-known icons are those in the Church of the Holy Savior and at the Saint Jovan Bigorski Monastery. Illuminated church records and writings, as well as textile work done by women, have also been preserved for centuries.

FOLK ARTS

Macedonian women have for centuries been known as extraordinary needleworkers. The embroidery on the national costumes of all of North Macedonia's ethnic peoples identifies them by location and background. Though people rarely wear their traditional costumes in daily life any more, each area and ethnic group has its own, and they are worn on holidays and during folkloric performances. Many of the costumes for both men and women have headpieces worked in elaborate embroidery and edged in lace. Both Muslim and Christian women covered their heads in 19th-century Macedonia with a large veil made of lace or embroidered net or cotton.

Embroidery work on the costumes is organized into repeating geometric and floral motifs. The cloth is made of linen with elaborate and dense stitching in wool or cotton. The colors of the costumes have significance for both the wearer and the people who watch. Red symbolizes love, bloodshed, and fire. Brown signifies stability and steadfastness, white signifies happiness and ease, and black signifies night and mystery. A stitch known as the Macedonian stitch, with rows that alternate between left-slanting stitches and right-slanting stitches, identifies work found in other countries, such as Greece and Canada, as coming from a Macedonian needleworker.

FOLK DANCING AND MUSIC

The *teskoto* (TESH-koh-toh), or the hard dance, is the traditional dance performed by the men of North Macedonia. Like circle dances in many cultures, the teskoto is a dance known to most of the men in the country. It is a dance that acknowledges the sorrow and difficulty of life and the awakening of the Macedonian national spirit. Facing each other in a circle, the men hold their hands high in the air and move to the slow, stately beat of a large cylindrical drum, called a *tapan* (TAH-pahn), and the *zurla* (ZUR-lah), a double-reed instrument like an oboe, with a keening moan. As the music accelerates, the men dance faster. The dance ends when the oldest dancer leaps onto the drum and kneels as the drummer slows the beat to a doleful stop.

A troupe of male dancers performs the *teskoto*, a traditional folk dance, in the western village of Galichnik in North Macedonia.

The teskoto is Macedonia's most famous and beloved dance. It is often performed for visitors by people dressed in their traditional ethnic or national costumes. However, it is just as likely to be performed spontaneously by a group of people at a wedding, a holiday feast, a street fair, or another festive occasion. With many young men leaving home to pursue work in other countries, it is sometimes performed as a farewell.

Macedonian dancers are usually accompanied by the tapan and one or more wind instruments. The *kaval* (KAH-vahl) is a pipe without a mouthpiece. The player blows across the edge of the opening, like blowing on a bottle. The length of the pipe determines the kaval's tone; the longer the pipe, the deeper the tone. Macedonian bagpipes, *gajda* (GAHJ-dah), contribute a characteristic drone to many festivities, and the two-stringed lute called a *tambura* (TAHM-boo-rah) can often be heard in the background. Often, the music is provided by Roma musicians.

LITERATURE

The North Macedonian literary tradition dates from the work of Saints Cyril and Methodius, who developed the precursor to the Macedonian alphabet in the ninth century. Their disciple, Saint Clement of Ohrid, translated Greek texts into Macedonian for the benefit of his people and was a gifted writer of poetry, songs, and sermons in his own right. Other writers from the period contributed lyrically beautiful religious prayers, hymns, sermons, and elucidations of religious texts. Throughout the Middle Ages, monks transcribed and illuminated religious texts and even preserved in writing some of the romances current among the people.

During the Ottoman occupation of the Balkans, Macedonian literature was largely confined to the monasteries, where it was restricted to the copying out of known texts. The writers of the first great wave of Macedonian literature were educated in the religious tradition of the early monks, and their writing continued in the religious vein. However, the works of Grigor Parlichev, including the poems "Skenderbeg" and "The Sirdar," broke ground for a new Balkan style of writing in the 19th century that celebrated folk and local heroes.

The bronze likeness of poet Grigor Parlichev is one of more than two dozen such sculptures of Macedonian artists and musicians featured on the Art Bridge, a pedestrian bridge spanning the Vardar River in Skopje.

Macedonian poetry of the 20th century began with the revolutionary poems of young men who wrote fervently as they fought occupying armies and died young. Koli Nedelkovske (1912—1941) wrote "Glas od Makadonija," a cry from the heart summoning fellow Macedonians to resist fascism. Koco Racin (1908—1943) also lived a hard, short life of poverty and revolutionary resistance. His book of poetry, published in 1939, *Beli Mugri* (*White Dawns*), was forbidden by the occupying forces of his homeland, but it was passed around from hand to hand by readers who loved it for its celebrations and observations of ordinary people. Its wide underground circulation had an enormous revolutionary impact, earning the poet the respect of his comrades. For the next four years, he continued to write, but his work also earned him the dedicated enmity of

Janaki Manaki (1878–1954) and his brother Milton (1880–1964), Macedonian photographers, were the first cameramen in the Balkans, and they used their craft to document their homeland's history. They established the Studio for Art Photography in Bitola in 1905. For the next few years, they won international renown, traveling and exhibiting in Paris, Vienna, and London. In London, Milton saw his first movie camera and found a new direction and medium. With a Bioscope camera, he brought cinematography to Macedonia.

The Manaki brothers began their cinematic record of Macedonian life with a film of their 114-year-old grandmother, a weaver in their hometown. Along the way, they recorded the lives and work of other weavers, weddings, religious rituals and celebrations, ethnic festivals and customs, and, importantly, the reprisals of the Turks against the Macedonians following the Ilinden Uprising. To show their films, they opened a movie theater.

A statue honoring Milton Manaki stands in Bitola.

In still photography, the brothers made a record of the first half of the 20th century. Their photographs preserve the images of the Balkan Wars and World War I, and continue beyond the liberation of Macedonia from the Nazis in 1944.

the occupiers, who pursued him for the rest of his life until his death on a mountain road in 1943.

Another notable—and longer-living—Macedonian writer of the 20th century was Slavko Janevski (1920—2000), who worked in both poetry and prose. His *Village Beyond the Seven Ash Trees,* dating from 1952, is viewed as the first Macedonian novel.

VISUAL ARTS

North Macedonia has a rich artistic life. More than 250 exhibitions of work by North Macedonian artists and guests from foreign countries are organized each year. The works of the Macedonian painters Nikola Martinoski, Lazar Lichenoski, Petar Mazev, Dimitar Kondovski, Petar Hadzi Boskov, Vangel Naumovski, Vasko Tashkovski, and Gligor Chemerski have been exhibited around the world.

PHOTOGRAPHY AND FILM

Movie theaters are everywhere in North Macedonia, showing a wide range of films in many languages and from many countries. Macedonian moviegoers

The 39th International Cinematographers' Film Festival took place in 2018 in Bitola.

THE MACEDONIAN SUN The Macedonian sun is a symbol of Macedonian culture that has been cherished for over 3,000 years. An eight-rayed or sixteen-rayed geometric rendition, sometimes called a star, has appeared on coins, costumes, flags, stamps, and religious icons. As a symbol of the ancient Macedonian kingdom, it has been found preserved on military equipment and

artwork. On medieval religious paintings of Mary, the mother of Jesus, the Macedonian sun decorates her head covering and her gown. Hammered gold boxes and tomb paintings testify to the importance of the sun as North Macedonia's symbol.

When Macedonia became an independent country in 1991, it proudly raised a flag with the sixteen-pointed sun, called the Vergina Sun. In 1992, to commemorate its independence, the Macedonian postal system issued a stamp with a picture of the flag. However, opposition from neighboring Greece forced the country to give up its claim to the Vergina Sun as its symbol.

THE MACEDONIAN LION Ancient historians have left records of the presence of lions in ancient Macedonia. Among warriors and courtiers, the lion hunt was a popular pastime and competition as recorded in recovered art and artifacts. One mosaic shows a Macedonian warrior taking part in a lion hunt wearing nothing but his cape and the distinctive Macedonian hat called a kausia

(kah-oo-SEE-yah). Macedonian kings also dressed in the lion's pelt, and an ancient coin shows a profile of Alexander the Great, his head topped with a lion's scalp.

In 338 BCE, when the Macedonians defeated the Greeks at Chaeronea in central Greece, they built a sculpture of a proud-standing lion on the battlefield. Throughout the centuries, families have identified themselves as Macedonian by incorporating the lion into their coats of arms.

are accustomed to seeing experimental and foreign films as well as dubbed and subtitled versions of Hollywood blockbusters.

In 1905, the brothers Milton and Janaki Manaki shot the first filmed material in the Balkans in their native town of Bitola and thus laid the foundations for film and photography in this region. The film industry flourished during Macedonia's days as a Yugoslav republic, partly owing to the reputation it had acquired as it built on the Manaki legacy of teaching and production. The years following independence were difficult, as technological changes were rapid and money was scarce. Still, there have been notable successes. The 1994 Macedonian film *Before the Rain*, directed by Milcho Manchevski, was nominated for the 1995 Academy Award for Best Foreign Language Film, after having previously won the Golden Lion at the Venice Film Festival.

The 2019 film *Honeyland*, directed by North Macedonia's Ljubomir Stefanov and Tamara Kotevska, won three awards at the 2019 Sundance Film Festival. It was also nominated for Best International Feature Film and Best Documentary at the 92nd Academy Awards in 2020. The documentary, in Turkish, profiles the

Directors Ljubomir Stefanov and Tamara Kotevska attend the 2019 premiere of their film *Honeyland* during the 2019 Sundance Film Festival in Utah.

The beautifully lit National Theater and the Museum of the Macedonian Struggle sit along the Vardar River in Skopje.

life of a female beekeeper in an isolated mountain village in North Macedonia. The movie garnered tremendous international praise. The *New York Times* called it "sublime and strange and full of human and natural beauty."

THEATER

Several professional theater companies are active in North Macedonia, presenting hundreds of performances each year. There is a Theater of the Nationalities in Skopje, consisting of Albanian and Turkish drama companies. There are also Romani theater companies.

The most successful theater companies are the Drama Theater and the Macedonian National Theater, both in Skopje; the National Theater, Bitola; and the Pralipe Romani Theater. These companies have been winners of a large number of the highest awards in the former Yugoslavia and also of many international prizes and acknowledgments. The Theater of the Nationalities, with its Albanian and Turkish drama companies, has also participated in many national and international theater festivals and has received high praise.

The founder of modern Macedonian theater is Vojdan Chernodrinski (*Macedonian Blood Wedding*, 1901). Goran Stefanovski is the author whose plays have been most frequently performed. There have been numerous productions of his plays in Macedonian, Serbo-Croatian, Slovene, English, French, Russian, German, Albanian, Turkish, Hungarian, Polish, Slovak, Romanian, and Greek.

Whimsical bronze sculptures depict historical and everyday figures throughout the city of Skopje.

INTERNET LINKS

https://honeyland.earth
The site for the film *Honeyland* includes a trailer.

https://www.manaki.com.mk
The site of the Manaki Brothers International Cinematographers' Film Festival is presented in English.

https://www.myguidemacedonia.com/travel-articles/traditional -macedonian-folk-dances
Various videos present the folk dances and music of North Macedonia.

https://www.nytimes.com/2019/07/15/world/europe/macedonia -church-of-st-george-restoration.html
The restoration of the ancient Church of Saint George in Kurbinovo is the subject of this article.

LEISURE

People enjoy a dip in the waters of Lake Ohrid.

11

NORTH MACEDONIA IS NOT A wealthy country, but people enjoy leisure time and recreation. As is true nearly everywhere, they relax with family and friends, watch TV, read the newspaper, and have hobbies. They have a tradition of making their own entertainment. Every town has its own festivals commemorating historical, religious, and ethnic events both tragic and triumphant. However, Macedonians are increasingly urban and youthful, and the pastimes of the 21st century, from online dating to mall shopping, are also a part of the scene.

MEDIA

Television is North Macedonia's most popular news medium, with the public broadcaster MRT and five national commercial stations dominating the ratings. There are many other cable and satellite channels available as well. Both radio and television broadcast in many languages, including Albanian, Turkish, Greek, Bulgarian, Romani, and Vlach. Macedonian television was the first to broadcast programs in Albanian.

Though North Macedonia is landlocked and has no ocean shoreline, it has plenty of beaches. Lake Ohrid offers numerous beaches that are all very popular with locals and tourists alike. The beaches at Lake Prespa are some of the best in the country, and the weather is often sunny. Most beaches are sandy, and the views are extraordinary.

The state-subsidized *Nova Makedonija* and *Vecer* are daily newspapers with sites available online as well. The private daily *Sloboden Pechat* is also available online. There are other dailies and weeklies as well, although some print papers have closed recently due to falling circulation.

In 2016, there were 1.475 million internet users, or more than 70 percent of the population. That number will most likely continue to grow.

SPORTS

Sports activities take place in more than 1,500 clubs with about 150,000 active members. The most popular sport is football (soccer), followed by basketball, handball, volleyball, wrestling, swimming, and karate.

Like soccer fans everywhere, North Macedonians play soccer wherever they can, in the street or in a club. They are also loyal fans to their teams. The national team plays its home matches at the Tose Proeski Arena in Skopje. The team has yet to qualify for a World Cup tournament as of early 2020.

Elif Elmas of North Macedonia (in red) attempts to keep the ball from Poland's Przemyslaw Frankowski in the UEFA Euro 2020 qualification match in Skopje. However, Frankowski scored a goal, and Poland won the game by a 2-0 score.

When independent Macedonia first competed at the Olympic Summer Games in 1996, it was forced to carry the name Former Yugoslav Republic of Macedonia, due to the naming dispute with Greece. Since then, it has competed in every Summer and Winter Games as such; however in future Olympics, beginning with the 2020 Tokyo Games, the country's team will carry the name North Macedonia.

In 2004, runners carried the Olympic flame through western Macedonia on its way to the Summer Olympic Games in Athens, Greece. While it was a part of Yugoslavia, Macedonians competed as part of the Yugoslav team, but since independence, it has sent athletes to compete in swimming, wrestling, kayaking, canoeing, shooting, and boxing. Mogamed Ibragimov won the first Olympic medal for Macedonia since its independence when he brought home the bronze medal in wrestling from the 2000 Olympics in Sydney. As of early 2020, it remains the only medal the country has won, though numerous Macedonian athletes won medals in earlier Olympics competing for Yugoslavia.

A couple bikes in a city park in Skopje.

OUTDOOR RECREATION

North Macedonia's tiny size and varied landscape gives its people opportunities to take part in an amazing variety of outdoor activities. Swimming, water skiing, hiking, bicycling, and boating of all kinds are very popular in the mountain and lake districts. Divers in Lake Ohrid can explore a sunken village. Even people in the cities are rarely more than a half hour's drive from the mountains, where they can climb, camp, hunt, or just sit and take in the surrounding landscape. Mountaineering is the most popular outdoor sport, not surprising in a country that is 80 percent mountainous. Throughout the country, mountain hostels cater to the needs of mountaineers, providing dormitory sleeping for tired climbers.

The sport of caving, or spelunking, in North Macedonia has an international reputation. Just outside Prilep, on the way to Modriste, is an area of caves and underground tunnels where people once lived in complex communities dependent on each other for defense. Today, the tunnels are being studied, like others around the country, for their archaeological significance.

Winter activities include skiing, ice fishing, and winter camping. January and February are the best skiing months, and like hikers, skiers are never far from a mountain.

As conflicts in the area have diminished, tourism has begun to bring in outsiders who see potential in the beauty and variety of the North Macedonian outdoors. They have brought with them an appetite for things such as paragliding and orienteering that may be new to the area but have been quickly accepted.

A paraglider takes off from a mountain near the city of Prilep.

HOT SPRINGS

North Macedonia has several hot springs that provide medicinal baths. The water bubbles up from underground, passing through the minerals that give it its healing powers. Calcium, lime, and sulphur are the minerals of healing, and the smell of sulphur is a characteristic of the waters and the area around them. Some of the baths that have been built to use the water are only available to people with a doctor's prescription. Others are open to all and are beautiful examples of Turkish architecture. The Bansko Turkish Hot Springs near the Bulgarian border are one of the original Turkish baths. The Banjiste baths near the Albanian border are fed by three hot springs. In the morning, the baths are used for medicinal purposes and for physical therapy, but in the afternoon, they are open to all.

INTERNET LINKS

https://amateurtraveler.com/25-things-to-do-in-macedonia
This travel site lists recreational activities available to tourists and locals alike.

http://www.exploringmacedonia.com/home.nspx
This site publicizes the array of destinations and activities available in the country.

FESTIVALS

Someone dressed as a fantastical beast called a Kurent performs at the Prilep Carnival in 2018.

12

WITH A MAJORITY OF NORTH Macedonians being Orthodox Christians, holidays are scheduled according to the Orthodox calendar, which is based on the old Julian calendar. Orthodox Christian holidays thus fall a few weeks later than they do on the modern (Gregorian) calendar. For example, Orthodox Christmas falls on January 7. Roman Catholics observing Christmas on December 25 find they are in a small minority in North Macedonia. Similarly, Easter, which falls on a different date each spring, is also a little later in Orthodox practice. Both Orthodox Christmas and Easter are national holidays.

However, for the sizable Albanian Muslim minority, the government also recognizes Eid al-Fitr as a national holiday. That day, which marks the end of the Islamic holy month of Ramadan, falls on a different day each year as determined by the Islamic calendar.

Other national holidays in North Macedonia include patriotic commemorations. These are Republic Day, August 2, which marks the

Orthodox Christians in some countries, icluding Greece and Romania, have revised their calendar to celebrate Christmas on December 25, at the same time as Catholics and Protestants. However, North Macedonia, along with other predominantly Orthodox countries like Russia and Serbia, continues to mark the holiday on January 7. Some Macedonians like the idea of holding Christmas on December 25 and have asked the Macedonian Church to consider moving it, with no success.

Ilinden Uprising of 1903; Independence Day, September 8, which marks the day Macedonians voted to declare their independence from Yugoslavia; Day of the People's Uprising, October 11, which commemorates the 1941 uprising against the occupation by Axis forces (Germans, Italians, and Bulgarians); and Day of the Macedonian Revolutionary Struggle, October 23, which marks the founding of the Internal Macedonian Revolutionary Organization (IMRO) in 1893.

Saints Cyril and Methodius Day on May 24 is a public holiday that honors the saintly brothers and their gift of literacy. Saint Clement of Ohrid, a disciple of Cyril and Methodius, is celebrated on December 8, another public holiday.

NEW YEAR'S AND CHRISTMAS

In North Macedonia, New Year's Eve, December 31, is a festive time of twinkling outdoor lights, decorations, Christmas trees, fireworks, and outdoor concerts. New Year's Day is the time for gift giving.

A Christmas market lights up the main city square in downtown Skopje.

Strange and gory costumes are a must at the ancient Vevcani Carnival in the village of the same name in the Lake Ohrid region. The celebration is thought to date back 1,400 years and marks the Orthodox Saint Vasilij Day each January 13 (the first day of the old Julian calendar), which is also known as Old New Year. Though the festival celebrates a saint, it's rooted in pre-Christian traditions, as the costumes reflect. Many costumes are particularly ghoulish in a manner similar to those of Halloween. Participants frolic in the streets with merriment, enjoying food, wine, music, and bonfires. Masked performers may comment on current political events, but it's all in fun.

Costumed revelers are a macabre sight at the annual Vevcani Carnival.

A family attends Good Friday services at the Church of Saint Clement in Skopje.

Orthodox Christmas, held on January 7, has its own traditions, totally unrelated to Western-style Christmastime. The celebration begins the evening of January 5, which is called Kolede's Eve. Children go from door to door, singing Christmas carols or Kolede songs and receiving specially baked Kolede cookies, fruits, nuts, candy, or coins from their neighbors. The evening is a time for bonfires, and folks gather around them in festive fashion.

Christmas Day is a time for family and church. At Christmas dinner, the main dish is typically fish, as meat is not allowed. An oak branch may be the centerpiece, as oak symbolizes eternal life. An oak log may also be placed in the fireplace, and oak branches and leaves decorate the house. A traditional bannock bread baked with a coin hidden inside is broken into pieces, one for each member of the family and one for God. The person who finds the coin will be the luckiest in the coming year, but if the coin is in God's piece of bread, the best fortune will come to the entire family.

EASTER

Easter is the most important holiday for Christians in North Macedonia, celebrating the resurrection of Jesus Christ. The week before Easter is celebrated as Holy Week, and tradition guides each day. On Wednesday, people in Christian homes dye eggs red. They rise early to do this because of a belief that eggs painted before dawn hold special powers to protect the household against evil. On Friday (Good Friday), they do no hard work, not even cooking. They attend services in the church and fast in remembrance of the day Jesus died. Each person brings a flower and takes one home to bring good health. Saturday is the day of the funeral. Just before midnight, people come to the church carrying candles and red eggs. They parade three times around the church while singing. At midnight, the church bells resound, and the priest greets the people with the words "Christ is risen." The people respond, "He is

THE ILINDEN UPRISING

The Ilinden Uprising was a revolt against the Ottoman Empire on August 2, 1903. The date was chosen to align with Saint Ilijah's Day. According to legend, Saint Ilijah (Elijah) was taken to heaven in a chariot of fire. Organizers of the uprising found the symbolism of his death and his day to bode well for their rebellion. Throughout Macedonia, people revolted against Ottoman rule that day, and on August 3 proclaimed themselves the Republic of Krushevo. After only 10 days, the uprising was quelled by Turkish troops, who outnumbered the rebels 16 to 1. The hideous reprisals visited on the Macedonian population remain in memory and in photographs. Though the independent Republic of Krushevo had only a 10-day life, the revolutionary effort that brought it about remained a part of Macedonian identity throughout the 20th century. Today, August 2 is celebrated as a national holiday.

The Ilinden Memorial, or Makedonium, is dedicated to fighters and revolutionaries who participated in the Ilinden Uprising of 1903. The uniquely designed building is in Krushevo, the site of the event.

risen indeed," and the mourning period is over. Sunday is the day of celebration, and people go early to the church to receive Holy Communion. The celebration continues for three more days.

FOLK CUSTOMS

Folk customs are cherished in North Macedonia as a tribute to the past and a link to people who, though separated by borders, share the same beliefs and practices. In summer, festivals are held throughout the country in towns large and small, from Skopje to Ohrid to Tetovo.

Some of the holidays celebrated by Macedonians are related to the harvest cycle, like Saint Trifun's Day, when people go out to prune the grape vines in preparation for the new growth.

Duhovden, or Spirits' Day, is celebrated by Christians throughout the country on three days in June, usually beginning on a Sunday. The dates vary from year to year, but the first day is the most important. On that day, people clean the graves of their ancestors and cover them with walnut leaves. People bring food and drink to the church, sharing with their fellow parishioners in honor of the dead.

Saint Jovan's Day is celebrated at the Saint Jovan Bigorski Monastery. The first day of this two-day holiday is a day of fasting. In one house in the nearby village, a woman makes bread with flour bought with money from the church. When it is ready, she carries it to the monks at the monastery while the people from the village celebrate. In the evening, the people sit down together for a great feast, which the women have been preparing throughout the day. The priest blesses the water, and the people take it home with them, believing that it now has the power to heal. The evening is filled with music and dancing.

GALICHNIK WEDDING Near the city of Mavrovo is a tiny mountain village called Galichnik, a place with few year-round residents. However, every year in July, the village comes to life as visitors drive up a winding road into the mountains and then walk the final distance, mostly uphill in usually very hot weather, to attend the Galichnik Wedding. Here, high in the mountains, the poets say, is the place where time begins and ends.

For more than a hundred years, the conflicts that shook the Balkans made this area inhospitable for the young men working in the trades and crafts. As they do today, many emigrated, relocating to countries with more secure economies where they earned money to help support their families at home. Though they lived abroad, Galichnik retained a hold on their hearts, and most wanted to marry girls from home.

In order to maintain relationships, migrants began to come home at the same time every year, on Saint Peter's Day, the 12th of July, and it became a tradition that anyone who wished to marry would have their wedding then. Often, there would be as many as 50 weddings in Galichnik on Saint Peter's Day, with every wedding party supplying their own music: two drummers playing the tapan and two pipers playing the zurla. The celebrations lasted as long as a week.

A bride and groom exit a church after their wedding in the North Macedonian town of Galichnik.

Today, the Galichnik Wedding has one bride and groom, chosen to be the prince and princess of the festival, and just one pair of tapan and zurla players. Dancing, music, and traditional costumes and customs all come together at the Galichnik Wedding as people from around the country and around the world gather to refresh their memories and their spirits, responding to the words of an old folk song: "Wherever you may be, on Saint Peter's Day you come home." The music echoes throughout the mountains for the two days of the festival. As at so many Macedonian festivals, men dance the teskoto, the slow dance they call "the hard one," in recognition of the sorrowful and difficult course of Macedonian history.

STRUMICA CARNIVAL The end of February brings the Strumica Carnival, a festival of masks that has been celebrated in Strumica since at least 1670. Traditionally, as in many Christian countries, the carnival marked the beginning of Lent, which ushered in a six-week period of fasting for Christians. Today, it is a more secular festival to bid farewell to winter and welcome spring.

At the traditional Masked Ball, celebrants crown the carnival prince and princess. Thousands of masked people from Macedonia and other European countries march in the procession to the Masked Ball. The masks are brilliantly colored, and fireworks accompany the festivities.

The next day is the children's carnival and a whole day and night of festivities, including dancing, storytelling, and music with traditional costumes. The carnival concludes with visits to the homes of engaged women, who receive their masked guests and accept gifts and best wishes.

MUSIC FESTS

Festivals celebrating folk music, drama, fine arts, and ethnic traditions occur throughout Europe every summer. Many of the musicians and players travel all summer, performing at festivals throughout the continent. Several international cultural events and festivals are held each year in North Macedonia. One of the best known is the Ohrid Summer Festival of Music and Drama, in which renowned musicians from around the world take part. Ohrid is also the place where the Balkan Festival of Folk Song and Dance is held. The Struga Poetry Evenings, which every year brings around 200 poets from around 50 countries to Struga, is another important summer event. Skopje is host to the World Cartoon Gallery, the May Opera Evenings, and the MOT International Theater Festival.

In June, the tiny village of Dolneni holds its Festival of Folk Instruments and Songs. From all over Macedonia and other countries in Europe, musicians and listeners descend for an international music festival. Musicians dressed in national and ethnic costumes perform centuries' old songs on traditional instruments. Bagpipes, horns of all sorts, and stringed instruments ring out to the delight of an audience that is often as international as the performers.

Music doesn't stop when summer ends, however. October brings the Skopje Jazz Festival, which began in 1982. World-famous American and European jazz musicians are in attendance along with Latin American and African stars, as well as North Macedonian artists.

In the late autumn, the Taksirat Festival brings thousands of fans of alternative music to Skopje. Homegrown and well-known foreign artists perform punk, metal, rock, hip-hop, reggae, and indie music in an atmosphere of high-voltage fun.

INTERNET LINKS

http://ohridskoleto.com.mk/en
The site of the Ohrid Summer Festival has information in English as well as photos of past performers.

https://www.theatlantic.com/photo/2014/01/the-carnival-of -vevcani/100661
Photos of the Vevcani Carnival reveal examples of the many artful homemade costumes.

https://www.timeanddate.com/holidays/macedonia
This calendar site lists the official national holidays and observances in North Macedonia.

FOOD

The roasted red pepper sauce *ajvar* is spread on two slices of bread.

13

FOOD CULTURE RARELY STOPS AT A country's border. The traditional cuisine of North Macedonia is similar, if not identical, to that of the other countries in the Balkan region. It reflects the influence of history and the many ethnic groups that played a part in it. Stuffed grape leaves, for example, show a Greek influence, while burek, a savory, layered pie with a phyllo-dough crust and various fillings, resembles dishes known by other names throughout the Balkans. Easter breads and other pastries associated with holidays appear in the cuisines of many countries that share religious beliefs and customs. Also, the Macedonian love of thick, rich Turkish coffee is from the days of Ottoman rule.

The fruits, vegetables, and grains that grow best in a certain climate are typically well represented in a country's cuisine. North Macedonia's warm, Mediterranean and continental climate is excellent for growing

Ajvar is a beloved condiment in North Macedonia and throughout the Balkans. It is a reddish, saucy relish made of roasted red bell peppers, vinegar, oil, paprika, and garlic, and it is served with meats, cheeses, and breads. It can be mild or hot, and it may contain eggplant or tomatoes.

A Burger King stand in the food hall at Skopje International Airport attests to the cosmopolitan nature of the city.

a wide variety of crops. The country's dairy industry produces yogurt and sirene cheese, a brined, white, feta-like cheese that is sprinkled liberally over many dishes, including *shopska*, a fresh salad.

Traditional meals may be associated with home and family, but the food culture of North Macedonia is not immune to modern international influences as well. Shopping malls and urban centers in Skopje and other cities feature pizza, hamburgers, and tacos like any mall or city in North America or Western Europe.

TRADITIONAL FOODS

Balkan food is traditionally meat-heavy. Longtime favorites include hearty stews, stuffed vegetables—especially meat- and rice-stuffed cabbage, grape leaves, peppers, eggplant, and zucchini—and bean dishes. Meat (pork, chicken, lamb, and beef) and fish are served with rice, pasta, and vegetables—

typically eggplant, beans, cucumbers, mushrooms, peppers, potatoes, and tomatoes. Moussaka, borrowed from Greek cuisine, is a popular casserole in North Macedonia, where it is typically made with minced beef and potato or eggplant. Other minced meat dishes include meatballs and *kjebapchinja* (kye-BAHP-chee-nya), a Macedonian sausage of beef and lamb.

Some traditional foods of North Macedonia make for a tempting spread.

THE BEAN POT

For Macedonian Christians who observe Orthodox traditions, Friday is a day of abstinence from eating meat. The meal that night might well be *tavce gravce* (TAHV-cheh GRAH-cheh), a baked bean dish often called the national dish. The name literally means "beans cooked in a pan," from the Turkish word *tava*, or "pan." Similar bean stews or soups with different names—including *pasulj*, *prebranac*, and *grah*—are found in the other countries of the former Yugoslavia.

In North Macedonia, the tradition is to cook the beans in a clay pot. In fact, earthenware pots for this purpose are still produced. Veles, a town in the center of the country, and Vranestica to the west were historically well-known for clay pot production. The artisan-based industry nearly died out when cheaper imports became available, but a resurgence of appreciation for homemade crafts has reinvigorated the potters and their pottery.

Although recipes vary, tavce gravce usually features beans and onions, and sometimes peppers and tomatoes. North Macedonia is especially known for its variety of peppers, which are featured in many traditional dishes. When abstaining from meat is not an issue, sausages are often added to tavce gravce.

DESSERTS AND DRINKS

Desserts in North Macedonia include fruit salads, puddings, cakes, and pastries. Excellent fresh fruits are available in season. Most are grown on small family farms without chemical treatment. Strong Turkish coffee, sometimes called Macedonian coffee, is served in all homes, as well as in restaurants and cafés. Wine, beer, and soft drinks are produced locally.

Fresh fruits and vegetables create a colorful and healthful picture at a grocery market street display in Ohrid.

One of the most popular desserts in North Macedonia is called baklava. This heavy, honey-drenched dessert is made mostly in winter. The classic filling is made with layers of phyllo dough alternating with ground walnuts and cinnamon. Many other cake or pastry desserts are similarly drenched in a honey syrup—another Ottoman influence. Turkey is also the origin of another, simpler favorite dessert called *sutlijas* (SUHT-lee-yash), or rice pudding.

Baklava is a favorite dessert throughout the region.

INTERNET LINKS

https://www.buzzfeed.com/jovcov/delicious-macedonian-dishes-for-your-inner-foodie-h04v
Photos and descriptions of 22 North Macedonian dishes are presented on this site.

https://www.discoveringmacedonia.com/2019/macedonian-food-everything-you-need-to-know
This travel site has a section on Macedonian foods.

TAVCE GRAVCE (BAKED BEANS)

This dish, which translates as "beans in a pan" is said to be the national dish of North Macedonia.

1 pound (450 grams) dry white beans
   (great northern, cannellini, or lima)
½ teaspoon baking soda
2 bay leaves
1 onion, peeled and cut into quarters
2 tablespoons cooking oil
2 medium onions, thickly sliced
4 garlic cloves, chopped
1 or 2 (to taste) green chili peppers,
   finely chopped
2 bell peppers, red and/or yellow, sliced
1 or 2 tablespoons paprika
A few fresh mint leaves, chopped (or 1 teaspoon dried mint)
Salt and pepper to taste

Soak the beans for 8 hours or overnight with ½ teaspoon of baking soda. Rinse and drain.

Add beans to large pot; add the first onion and the bay leaves. Cover with water, bring to a boil, cover pot, and turn down to a simmer. Cook according to bean package directions or until firm but soft. Drain beans and onion mixture, and set aside, reserving cooking liquid.

Preheat oven to 400°F (205°C).

In a frying pan over medium heat, sauté the other onions and peppers in the oil until slightly soft. Add garlic, and sauté 1 more minute. Add paprika, and cook just about 10 seconds to bloom flavor. Remove pan from heat so as not to burn the paprika, and add to beans mixture. Add salt and pepper to taste.

Pour bean mixture into an oiled clay pot or any casserole dish. Add enough reserved cooking liquid to barely cover the beans. Bake about 1 hour, checking occasionally. If beans are drying out, add more liquid. Beans are done when a crust forms on top. Sprinkle with mint.

SHOPSKA (MACEDONIAN SALAD)

This salad is popular throughout the Balkans.

4 tomatoes, chopped

2 cucumbers, peeled and chopped

1 red onion or three scallions, chopped

1 green pepper, chopped

2 tablespoons olive or sunflower oil

Drizzle of red wine vinegar (optional)

½ cup or more of sirine cheese or sheep's milk feta cheese, coarsely grated or crumbled

Parsley, chopped

Black olives, halved (optional)

Put the vegetables in a large serving bowl and drizzle with olive oil and vinegar. Mix gently. Cover with the cheese and garnish with parsley and olives.

Serve immediately.

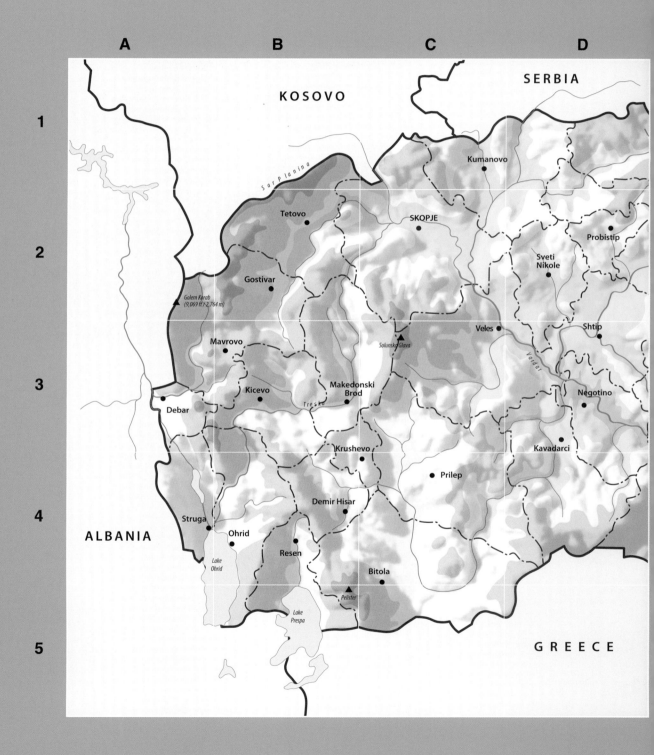

A   B   C   D

1

KOSOVO   SERBIA

Sar Planina

Kumanovo

Tetovo   SKOPJE

2   Probistip

Gostivar   Sveti
Nikole

Golem Korab
(9,069 ft / 2,764 m)

Veles   Shtip

Mavrovo   Solunska Glava

3   Kicevo   Makedonski   Negotino
Brod

Treska

Debar   Kavadarci

Krushevo

Prilep

Demir Hisar

4   Struga

Ohrid

Resen   Bitola

Lake   Pelister
Ohrid

Lake
Prespa

5   GREECE

ALBANIA

Vardar

MAP OF NORTH MACEDONIA

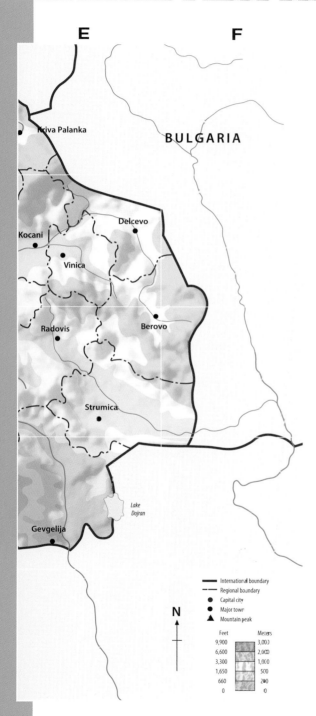

E   F

BULGARIA

Kriva Palanka

Delcevo

Kocani

Vinica

Radovis

Berovo

Strumica

Lake Dojran

Gevgelija

International boundary
Regional boundary
● Capital city
● Major town
▲ Mountain peak

N

Feet	Meters
9,900	3,000
6,600	2,000
3,300	1,000
1,650	500
660	200
0	0

Berovo, E3
Bitola, C4

Debar, A3
Delcevo, E2
Demir Hisar, B4

Gevgelija, E4
Golem Korab, A2
Gostivar, B2

Kavadarci, D3
Kicevo, B3
Kocani, E2
Kriva Palanka, E1
Krushevo, C4
Kumanovo, C1

Lake Dojran, E4
Lake Ohrid, B4—B5
Lake Prespa, B5

Makedonski Brod,
  B3
Mavrovo, B3

Negotino, D3

Ohrid, B4

Pelister, B5
Prilep, C4
Probistip, D2

Resen, B4
Radovis, E3

Sar Planina, B1
Shtip, D3
Skopje, C2
Solunska Glava, C3
Struga, A4
Strumica, E3
Sveti Nikole, D2

Tetovo, B2
Treska River, B3

Vardar River, D3
Veles, C3
Vinica, E2

ECONOMIC NORTH MACEDONIA

Farming

Tobacco

Services

Airport

Tourism

Natural Resources

Fishing

Lignite

Manufacturing

Food Processing

Hydroelectricity

Metals

Oil Refining

Textiles

Thermoelectric Plants

ABOUT THE ECONOMY

All figures are 2017 estimates unless otherwise noted.

GROSS DOMESTIC PRODUCT (GDP, OFFICIAL EXCHANGE RATE)
$11.37 billion

GDP PER CAPITA
$14,900

LABOR FORCE
950,800

CURRENCY
1 denar (MKD) (plural, denari)
$1 (USD) = 56.11 MKD
Notes: 10, 50, 100, 200, 500, 1,000 denari
Coins: 1, 2, 5, 10, 50 denari

POPULATION BELOW POVERTY LINE
21.5 percent (2015)

GDP BY SECTOR
agriculture 10.9 percent, industry 26.6 percent, services 62.5 percent

UNEMPLOYMENT RATE
22.4 percent

NATURAL RESOURCES
iron ore, copper, lead, zinc, chromite, manganese, nickel, tungsten, gold, silver, asbestos, gypsum, timber

AGRICULTURAL PRODUCTS
grapes, tobacco, vegetables, fruits, milk, eggs

EXPORTS
foods, beverages, tobacco, textiles, miscellaneous manufactured goods, iron, steel, automotive parts

IMPORTS
machinery and equipment, automobiles, chemicals, fuels, food products

EXPORT PARTNERS
Germany 46.7 percent, Bulgaria 6.1 percent, Serbia 4.4 percent, Belgium 4.1 percent

IMPORT PARTNERS
Germany 11.9 percent, United Kingdom 10 percent, Greece 8 percent, Serbia 7.1 percent, China 5.9 percent, Italy 5.5 percent, Turkey 4.5 percent, Bulgaria 4.3 percent

CULTURAL NORTH MACEDONIA

Mavrovo National Park
The park has 300 square miles (780 sq km) of beautiful and protected mountain scenery. It is also the site of Golem Korab, North Macedonia's highest peak.

Saint Jovan Bigorski (John the Baptist) Monastery
This monastery complex in Mavrovo, which dates back to the 11th century, is famous for its beautiful wood carvings done in traditional Macedonian style.

Skopje
The many cultural and historic monuments in the old part of the city can be accessed by crossing the Kameni Most. It is a stone bridge built by the Romans, then again by the Turks over the Vardar in the first half of the 15th century.

Prehistoric Settlement
Debar, in western North Macedonia, is the site of a prehistoric settlement and a launching spot for rebellions against the Turks in the ninth century.

Lake Debar
The springs at this lake offer mineral water believed to have medicinal properties, supposedly curing various illnesses and skin conditions.

Krushevo
North Macedonia's highe[st] town is the site of the 1[0] day government forme[d] by the 1903 Ilinde[n] Insurrection. Resider[ts] preserve the memory of th[e] uprising by having colorf[ul] celebrations on August 2[.]

Struga Poetry Evenings
The town of Struga, a Neolithic settlement on the Via Egnatia, is now known as the capital of North Macedonian poetry and home of the yearly Struga Poetry Evenings festival.

Lake Ohrid
Estimated to be more than 3 million years old, the lake is the deepest lake in tbe Balkans and home of the Ohrid trout.

Galicica
Located between Lakes Ohrid and Prespa, the mountain has underground and underwater caves with stalactites and stalagmites.

Ohrid
The city, which along with the lake has UNESCO World Heritage status, is the site of the first university in the Balkans, the Ohrid Literary School.

Heraclea Lyncestis
Ruins of this fourth-century city in Bitola, which was founded on the Roman road the Via Egnatia, include a theater, basilicas, a forum, and intricate floor mosaics.

All figures are 2018 estimates unless otherwise noted.

COUNTRY NAME
Republic of North Macedonia

GOVERNMENT TYPE
Parliamentary republic

CAPITAL
Skopje

POPULATION
2,118,950

POPULATION GROWTH RATE
0.19 percent

URBANIZATION
58.2 percent (2019)

ETHNIC GROUPS
Macedonian 64.2 percent, Albanian 25.2 percent, Turkish 3.8 percent, Romani 2.7 percent, Serb 1.8 percent, other 2.3 percent (2002)
Note: North Macedonia has not conducted a census since 2002; Romani populations are usually underestimated in official statistics and may represent 6.5 to 13 percent of North Macedonia's population.

RELIGIONS
Macedonian Orthodox 64.8 percent, Muslim 33.3 percent, other Christian 0.4 percent, other and unspecified 1.5 percent (2002)

LANGUAGES
Macedonian (official) 66.5 percent, Albanian 25.1 percent, Turkish 3.5 percent, Romani 1.9 percent, Serbian 1.2 percent, other (includes Vlach and Bosnian) 1.8 percent (2002)
Note: Minority languages are co-official with Macedonian in municipalities where they are spoken by at least 20 percent of the population.

LIFE EXPECTANCY AT BIRTH
Total population: 75.9 years
Male: 73.8 years
Female: 78.2 years

INFANT MORTALITY RATE
7.8 deaths per 1,000 live births

LITERACY
Total population: 97.8 percent
Male: 98.8 percent
Female: 96.8 percent (2015)

TIMELINE

IN NORTH MACEDONIA	IN THE WORLD
	753 BCE
ca. 653 BCE	Rome is founded.
King Perdiccas I establishes the Macedonian kingdom.	
336–323 BCE	
The reign of Alexander the Great is when Macedonia reaches the peak of its military power.	
215–167 BCE	
Macedonia falls under Roman rule.	**600 CE**
855–886 CE	The height of the Mayan civilization is reached.
Brothers Cyril and Methodius create the Slavic alphabet and spread Christianity.	
1018	
The Macedonian Empire falls under Byzantine rule.	**1054**
1394	The Great Schism divides the Catholic Church into Eastern and Western churches—
Macedonia falls under five-century Turkish rule.	Orthodox Catholic and Roman Catholic.
	1530
	The transatlantic slave trade is organized by the Portuguese in Africa.
	1776
	US Declaration of Independence is signed.
	1789–1799
1903	The French Revolution takes place.
The Ilinden Uprising takes place.	
1912–1913	
The First and Second Balkan Wars occur. Macedonian territory is split among Bulgaria, Serbia, and Greece.	**1914–1918**
	World War I takes place.
1915	
Bulgaria occupies Macedonia.	**1939–19145**
1944	World War II takes place.
Proclamation of the Macedonian state occurs.	
1967	
Archbishopric of Ohrid is restored; proclamation of Macedonian Orthodox Church occurs.	**1969**
	US astronaut Neil Armstrong becomes first human on the moon.

IN NORTH MACEDONIA	IN THE WORLD
1991	**1991**
Macedonia declares independence.	Breakup of the Soviet Union takes place.
1993	
Macedonia is admitted to the United Nations.	
1995	
Greek objections force Macedonia to change flag.	
2001	**2001**
NLA ethnic Albanian militia group attacks government troops, setting off months of conflict. Government and rebels sign Ohrid peace treaty.	Al-Qaeda terrorists stage 9/11 attacks in New York; Washington, DC; and Pennsylvania.
2004	**2003**
Macedonia submits application to join EU.	War in Iraq begins.
2006	
Nikola Gruevski of the VMRO-DPMNE becomes prime minister.	
2008	**2008**
Greece blocks a NATO invitation to Macedonia over objections to the country's name. Snap elections are called.	The United States elects first African American president, Barack Obama.
2011	**2009**
Census is scrapped due to political disagreements.	Outbreak of H1N1 flu occurs around the world.
2015	**2015–2016**
Revelation of Gruevski's wiretap scheme triggers political crisis.	ISIS launches terror attacks in Belgium and France.
2015–2018	
Protesters demand government accountability.	
2017	**2017**
Social Democrat leader Zoran Zaev becomes prime minister.	Donald Trump becomes US president. Hurricanes devastate Houston, Caribbean islands, and Puerto Rico.
2018	**2018**
Greece and Macedonia sign Prespa Agreement. Gruevski flees country to avoid imprisonment.	Winter Olympics are held in South Korea.
2019	**2019**
Name change to North Macedonia comes into effect.	Notre Dame Cathedral in Paris is damaged by fire.

GLOSSARY

autocephalous
Independent, or having its own head.

balkanize
To knowingly assemble a group of people who have differing, usually incompatible, goals.

basilica
A Christian church built on Roman design with a central nave.

euthrophication
An excess of nutrients in a body of water, which can ultimately kill off animal life.

fresco
A painting, usually religious, executed on wet plaster walls and ceilings.

Glagolitic
The first Slavic script invented by Saints Cyril and Methodius.

icon
A stylized painting of a religious image used in the Eastern Orthodox Church.

Sarplaninac (shar-plan-EEN-atz)
A Macedonian sheepdog.

Shqip
The official Albanian language.

tapan
A double-headed drum played with mallets in Macedonian folk music.

tavce gravce (TAHV-cheh GRAH-cheh)
A baked bean entree often called the national dish of North Macedonia.

teskoto
A slow men's dance called "the hard one."

UXO
Unexploded ordnance; mines and bombs set or dropped during armed conflict that remain on site after the conflict ends.

Vergina Sun
A 16-rayed sunburst (or star) design from ancient Macedon, claimed as a symbol by both Greece and North Macedonia.

zurla (ZUR-lah)
A double-reeded folk instrument.

FOR FURTHER INFORMATION

BOOKS

Evans, Thammy. *North Macedonia.* 6th ed. Chalfont Saint Peter, UK: Bradt Travel Guides, 2019.

Lonely Planet. *Western Balkans.* 3rd ed. Melbourne, Australia: Lonely Planet, 2019.

Sheppard, Ruth. *Alexander the Great at War.* Oxford, UK: Osprey Publishing, 2008.

ONLINE

Balkan Insight. North Macedonia. https://balkaninsight.com/macedonia-home.

BBC News. "North Macedonia Country Profile." https://www.bbc.com/news/world-europe-17550407.

CIA. *The World Factbook.* "North Macedonia." https://www.cia.gov/library/publications/the-world-factbook/geos/mk.html.

Encyclopedia Britannica. "North Macedonia." https://www.britannica.com/place/North-Macedonia.

Euronews. North Macedonia. https://www.euronews.com/tag/north-macedonia.

ExploringMacedonia.com. http://www.exploringmacedonia.com.

MUSIC

Adam Good. *Dances of Macedonia and the Balkans*, 2002.

Strune. *Traditional Music From Macedonia*, Arc Music, 2003.

FILMS

Before the Rain. Directed by Milcho Manchevski. Criterion Collection, 1994.

Honeyland. Directed by Tamara Kotevska, Ljubo Stefanov. Dogwoof, 2019.

BIBLIOGRAPHY

Assembly of the Republic of North Macedonia. https://www.sobranie.mk/home-en.nspx.

BBC News. "North Macedonia Country Profile." https://www.bbc.com/news/world-europe-17550407.

CIA. *The World Factbook.* "North Macedonia." https://www.cia.gov/library/publications/the-world-factbook/geos/mk.html.

Encyclopedia Britannica. "North Macedonia." https://www.britannica.com/place/North-Macedonia.

Euronews. "North Macedonia." https://www.euronews.com/tag/north-macedonia.

European Commission. "North Macedonia 2019 Report." May 29, 2019. https://ec.europa.eu/neighbourhood-enlargement/sites/near/files/20190529-north-macedonia-report.pdf.

Freedom House. "Freedom in the World 2019: North Macedonia." https://freedomhouse.org/report/freedom-world/2019/north-macedonia.

Friedman, Victor A. "The Name's Macedonia. North Macedonia." *Foreign Affairs*, October 1, 2018.

Garding, Sarah E. "North Macedonia: In Brief." Congressional Research Service, May 29, 2019. https://fas.org/sgp/crs/row/R45739.pdf.

Global Security. "Macedonia—Ohrid Framework Agreement (OFA)." https://www.globalsecurity.org/military/world/europe/mk-ohrid.htm.

Jakov Marusic, Sinisa. "Macedonia Church Rules Out Moving Christmas." *Balkan Insight*, December 24, 2010. https://balkaninsight.com/2010/12/24/macedonian-church-hard-against-moving-christmas-celebration.

Karajkov, Risto. "Census Fails in Macedonia." *Osservatorio Balcani e Caucaso Transeuropa*. https://www.balcanicaucaso.org/eng/Areas/North-Macedonia/Census-fails-in-Macedonia-105372.

O'Hara, Megan. "The 10 Best Festivals in Macedonia." *The Culture Trip*, February 9, 2017. https://theculturetrip.com/europe/macedonia/articles/the-10-best-festivals-in-macedonia.

Radio Free Europe/Radio Liberty. "Pope Praises North Macedonia as 'Bridge Between East And West'." May 7, 2019. https://www.rferl.org/a/pope-francis-arrives-in-north-macedonia/29925552.html.

Synovitz, Ron. "Will Macedonia's Orthodox Church Also Break Away?" Radio Free Europe/Radio Liberty, October 18, 2018. https://www.rferl.org/a/29551213.html.

UNESCO World Heritage Convention. "Natural and Cultural Heritage of the Ohrid Region." https://whc.unesco.org/en/list/99.

INDEX

INDEX